WORD ^{OF} MOUTH

A Guide To Commercial Voice-Over Excellence

REVISED EDITION

Susan Blu and Molly Ann Mullin

POMEGRANATE PRESS, LTD.

Los Angeles - London

This is a Pomegranate Press, Ltd. book.

Word of Mouth

The Library of Congress Catalog Card Number is 87-061591

ISBN 0-938817-32-9

For Pomegranate Press, Ltd.

Publisher/Editor: Kathryn Leigh Scott
Creative Director/Book Design: Ben Martin
Xerox Ventura Publisher Consultants:
Jesse Berst, Leroy Chen
Cover Design: Jane Guthrie
Photographs: Ben Martin

Printed and Bound in the United States of America
by McNaughton and Gunn of Saline, Michigan.

Pomegranate Press, Ltd.
Post Office Box 17217
Beverly Hills, California 90209-3217

WORD OF MOUTH

To: My Mom and Dad, and to all the "people" who live inside me
Susan

To: My Dad, and to all those whose word of mouth is "love"
Molly Ann

ACKNOWLEDGMENTS

The authors wish to gratefully acknowledge the many people who contributed so willingly and generously to this book.

Our deep appreciation to: June Allyson, Jack Angel, Allison Argo, Paul Armbruster, Edward Asner, Larry Belling, Bobbi Block, Kathi Brandt, Greg Callahan, Nancy Cartwright, Cathy Cavadini, Cam Clarke, Philip L. Clarke, Sid Conrad, Elaine Craig, Brian Cummings, John B. Curtis, Jeff Danis, Jennifer Darling, Diane Davenport, Donna Lee Davies, Smae Spaulding Davis, Flo Di Re, Pat Fraley, Linda Gary, Dick Gautier, Gordon Hunt, Marcia Hurwitz, Gordon Jump, Kathy and Eric King of Photoking Labs, Paul Kirby, Jonathan Kirsch, Linda Kwan, Michael Laskin, Kathy Levin, Mary McDonald Lewis, Robert T. Lloyd, Sherry Lynn, Roger Marks, Ginny McSwain, David Meyer, Robert Morse, Pat Musick, Nicholas Omana, Patrick Pinney, Thom Pinto, Pam Predisik, Robert Ridgely, Marcy Robin, Andrea Romano, Sandie Schnarr, Michael Sheehan, Arlene Thornton, Rita Vennari, Lea Vernon, B. J. Ward, Jill Wayne, Beau Weaver, Libby Westby, John Westmoreland, Betty White.

We would also like to thank entertainment attorney, Sam Sacks, copyright attorney, Paul D. Supnik, and publishers, Kathryn Leigh Scott and Ben Martin for their contributions and support.

A special thanks to all those who have provided comfort and courage along the way. They include: Hazel M. and John Harrison Blu, J.W. (Bud) Mullin, Marian M. Hancock, Al Martin, Richard Rosen and many other dear (and tolerant!) friends whom we love very deeply.

CONTENTS

Susan Blu

Molly Ann Mullin

INTRODUCTION

WE: Hello! Welcome to the Wonderful World of Voice-Overs!

YOU: Who said that?

WE: We did.

YOU: Who is we?

WE: Susan Blu and Molly Ann Mullin.

YOU: Oh.

WE: We wrote this book.

YOU: I see. Um...?

WE: What's on your mind?

YOU: Who are Susan Blu and Molly Ann Mullin?

WE: Good question. And perhaps the very best place to start.

Susan Blu is a veteran of stage and screen work. In recent years, however, the majority of her income has come from doing voice-overs. Her numerous animation credits as an actor include such shows as SCOOBY-DOO, FLINTSTONE KIDS, and SMURFS for Hanna-Barbera; MY LITTLE PONY, TRANSFORMERS, and JEM for Sunbow; and GHOSTBUSTERS and BRAVESTAR for Filmation. Susan's commercial credits include National Milk Advisory Board (Spokeswoman), Zody's (Spokeswoman), Bank of America, Pepsi, and promos for ABC. Susan has been an animation dialogue director for several years. Some of her credits include TEENAGE MUTANT NINJA TURTLES, for Fred Wolf Films, THE WIZARD OF OZ, WALDO, THE NEW KIDS ON THE BLOCK for Dic Productions, THE NEW ADVENTURES OF HE-MAN, for Jet Lag Productions, and many more. Susan also teaches both commercial and animation voice-over workshops throughout the country.

These days Molly Ann Mullin works only part time in the field of commercial voice-overs. "Just enough to keep my mouth in it," she says. As a professional writer, she has penned over twenty plays for radio, television and stage, and has won several national awards for dramatic and comedic writing. Molly Ann is a member of the Dramatists Guild, the American Community Theatre Association, and is past President of the NBC Writers Workshop. She is a volunteer voice artist for Recording for the Blind, Inc., and is currently working on a novel.

What is a voice-over? A commercial voice-over is the audio portion of a radio or television sales or promotional spot. That is an industry definition, and now that you know it, you can forget it — except for those times when your puzzled friends and relatives want to know why you are making all those strange noises.

Our definition is one which focuses on you, the artist. We like to say that voice-over is the opportunity for you to look inside yourself, to find and become all the different people you already are. A voice-over is not just someone reading a commercial — it is a particular person, in a particular situation, talking to another particular person (or persons), about a particular product.

Notice we said you become certain people. Voice-over excellence requires acting in the finest sense of the word. Don't panic, all you non-actors out there. All this means is that to deliver believable ad copy, you must get in touch with the reality of the Speaker, as well as the circumstances surrounding him or her. And we'll show you how to do just that. Remember, even if the Speaker you are asked to do is described in the minutest detail — down to freckles, frown and flat feet — the Speaker you actually become is still just one of those many people you already have inside you. We'll help you find them, too. If you enjoy meeting new people, you'll love the discoveries you're going to make.

Now we'd like you to do a bit of soul-searching. Take a moment and answer this question — honestly: Why are you interested in voice-overs? — To make piles of money — To do something different — People have said you have an interesting voice, but you don't know what to do with it — You're a ham, but there's not enough pork in you to go in front of a camera. These and other reasons are valid. Just know what your choice is so you can focus on it for motivation during the tough times.

Our purpose is to give you the information you need to function as an excellent voice-over artist. Although this book is basically an introduction to the world of voice-overs, the techniques and methods we discuss work just as well for the seasoned professional as for the beginner.

How can a career in voice-overs begin? Molly Ann enrolled in Susan's voice-over classes just for fun. "I wanted to play with the spoken rather than the written word for a change, and you couldn't get me up on a stage or in front of a camera if you took my whole family hostage." With that first class, Molly Ann was hooked.

Susan had an active career as actress, singer and cabaret performer when she got a call from her agent. "If you were the Pillsbury Dough Girl, what would you sound like?" At that point, Susan didn't even know what a voice-over was. She thought for a moment, envisioned the role, and "a voice just came out." She was selected to be the official Pillsbury Dough Girl with a lucrative two-year contract. Susan freely credits her ignorance for a large portion of her early voice-over success. "I didn't know it could be difficult, so I never thought I couldn't do it. As I became more experienced, I started hearing the stories about how tough it could be. Rather than believe them, I started to study and get into classes to learn voice-over techniques, which I still practice every day."

With practice you, too, can acquire a positive, professional attitude and develop the excellent skills that will lead to a successful and rewarding career in voice-overs. And, while we are delighted that you are reading and using this book, and perhaps listening to the audiocassette we've produced to accompany it, we heartily encourage you to get to the point where you can finally put these tools down, walk away from them, and just go forth and do voice-overs. The workbook and tape will always be available for reference, but you must develop your own skills and instincts and trust your own feelings about this business. Beware the voice-over teachers who insist that you sign up for class after class after class. It is not you they are reluctant to let go of. It is your checkbook.

Our approach is a very positive one. We believe that the time and energy people spend dwelling on the negatives (I can't; I'm afraid; I'll never get this; etc.) are wasted. If people were to spend the same time and energy on the positives, they would soon achieve excellence in the field of voice-over work. We like to keep the entire learning process a game and not think of it as a goal. Goals tend to focus on the result, and they leave little or no room for the process, which is where the real fun and creativity take place. Games keep you in the process and out of the result. We will be making this point again and again because we firmly believe that if you concentrate on and stay in the process, the desired results will automatically come. If you aren't having fun doing voice-overs, do yourself a favor and get out of the business. The least bit of boredom or unhappiness will show up in your voice and everyone will be aware of it. A camera does not lie and neither does a microphone. Winning the game is important. Getting an agent or getting that job really do matter. But winning traditionally signals the end of the game. According to voice actor Jack Angel, in voice-overs you win by simply choosing to play the game. So treat each step you take to acquire and maintain voice-over excellence as a game — a fun place to visit — then move on to the next step and enjoy it for a while, too, before you move on to the next step and the next. And now ... let the games begin!

Chapter One

How To Begin

Approaching anything new, we often bring with us certain misconceptions. Let's begin by destroying five popular myths about the voice-over business.

1. Voice-overs are male-dominated.

If you were to keep track of how many commercials are done by men versus women, you would indeed find that the majority of spots are done by men. Wait, all you female voice-over students! Don't give up now. There's hope — and lots of it, too.

Ad agencies are becoming less and less tied to the concept that women can buy anything but they sure can't sell it. Some agency executives are very supportive of women artists in the voice-over field. Other executives, under pressure from clients who are tired of hearing the same male voices selling the same products again and again, are also actively looking for fresh new female talent.

Wait a minute, all you men out there! Don't you give up either. There's hope for you, too. Read on!

2. There is a clique in the industry.

This implies that the same people work all the time and there's no room for newcomers.

Let us re-emphasize that the search is definitely on for new voice-over people. And while the field is undoubtedly opening up to women, it is also in need of fresh new male talent.

Andrea Romano, former voice-over agent and current casting director at Hanna-Barbera, emphatically states: "There is always room in this business for anyone who has excellent animation and commercial talent."

Excellent talent — that's the key. Because there are so many of you who want to become professional voice-over artists, only the truly excellent will make it. And that's where the real clique is — a clique of excellence, not restricted to already-established talent. Anyone possessing voice-over excellence can get into the field.

Marvel Productions, Ltd. Recording Director Ginny McSwain draws on her background in casting, directing and agenting to add a word of caution: "Without being negative — you can make it — but realistically, you must be aware of how many people want to do voice-overs for a living, and how many artists are already paying mortgages from voice-overs alone. You must have a healthy insight into competition. Being in touch with your own voice, constantly practicing and training to hone your skills, plus having the strong desire to put your own vocal signature on the air can keep you in prime shape to win those jobs."

3. You need to have an unusual voice.

If you were blessed with the power of speech, you already have something about your natural voice that makes it different or special. In fact, your voice is unique; no one else has one identical to yours.

Given a large enough sample of phonemes (the sounds we use to make words), experts can use the vocal equivalent of fingerprints, called voice prints, to positively identify one speaker from all others. One of your first steps will be to find out what the "special something" in your voice is. People do get into this business because their voices "sound so different." They have an unusual accent or rhythm or pitch — and that gets them work. They are hot for a while, but many of these people do not last. Why? Because they don't bother to study and develop voice-over excellence.

They have hit on one way of delivering copy and they use it over and over again. When directed to change the delivery, they are at a loss. Once the novelty wears off, they are no longer in demand; those who can take direction and have developed vocal flexibility are the ones who have long-term voice-over careers.

A producer of many commercial spots, Nicholas Omana, says: "Flexibility is very important. Over the years, I've seen different vocal styles come and go. Yesterday it was the more aggressive hard sell. Today they want a softer, more laid-back approach. You must be able to change in order to keep working."

Using voice-over artist Thom Pinto, owner of Voicetrax West, as an example, Nicholas adds: "You know, even Thom says he doesn't have a great or unusual voice. He has an anonymous voice, but that man works all the time! He has the ability to meld his voice into many different characters. Producers never get tired of hearing him because he's always someone different. Even his close friends don't always recognize him in the spots he's done. The more versatile and chameleon-like you are, the more you will work."

Casting director Samantha Paris, who opened Sam's Place, a voice-over casting and training center in Sausalito, California, says, "At one time, voice-over was about having a good voice and knowing how to announce. But these days, commercials reflect what's popular on TV, and what's popular is 'real people,' or 'slice of life' type shows. But when a producer says he or she wants it to sound real, that doesn't mean an unpolished voice off the street. It takes a lot of skill to sound like an everyday person. Of course, if you happen to have an interesting or beautiful voice, that's a gift and it can sometimes work to your advantage, but it's not necessary."

Elaine Craig of Elaine Craig Voicecasting says, "Voice-over actors should have the flexibility to change their preconceived ideas of how the copy should be read when I give them various directions. For instance, I have directed actors who insist on reading the copy according to their own interpretation, closing their minds to my direction and therefore limiting their chances of landing the job. The ability to listen and interpret the given direction is often more important to me than the quality of their voice."

4. You have to be a certain age to do certain characters.

What age? Which characters? We believe that voice-over excellence does not involve "doing a sixty-year-old voice," for example. Rather, it involves becoming a particular sixty-year-old character. The appropriate voice will come automatically.

Voice-overs are delightfully ageless. Each voice has built-in physical characteristics that allow the artist to make certain age and sex crossovers. Susan has done a number of young-boy characters because of the lower pitch and natural crack in her voice. "Women have more opportunities here," she says. "Once a boy's voice has changed, chances are he can no longer produce a believable pre-adolescent male voice."

Producers prefer to cast adults to play children's parts, but they don't always think of a woman playing the part of a young boy. On one occasion there was a casting call for the role of a young boy. Susan's agent succeeded in persuading the producers to give Susan an audition. The agent's persistence paid off — Susan got the role. We encourage you to keep practicing and stretching to do characters of both sexes and, barring any physical limitations to your vocal range, you can create believable male and female characters of many different ages.

5. You must already be a professional actor.

Cunningham, Escott, Dipene and Associates Vice President Dona Lee Davies, whose background includes casting, production and agenting, says: "This is absolutely not true. Anyone who develops voice-over excellence can make it in this business. However, in order to develop voice-over excellence and to read well, you must learn to act." Those of you who wouldn't take an acting class at gunpoint are probably mentally packing your bags right now and taking the next plane out of here. Don't go! Hear us out. You can always catch a later flight.

Eventually you may decide to do a few acting workshops; they would be an excellent complement to your voice-over training. But a good voice-over class automatically includes an acting class.

Acting involves getting in touch with the reality of a particular person in a particular situation. What makes it real is you — reaching inside to draw on your own experience to become that person in that situation. And that's what voice-overs are all about.

Somewhere inside, you have stored everyone and everything you have ever experienced. In this business we are privileged to enter that treasure room, and sample and explore to our heart's delight. Inside, we discover and become a multitude of different people who have been there all along, just waiting for us to find them.

So much for the myths. We hope you can lay them to rest, for believing them will only give them the power to exist. And, existing, they will leave no room in your world for voice-over success. Now that you are open to success, let's look at what it takes to launch your voice-over career. First, there are the physical essentials:

1. A voice.

Just having one is not enough. What you choose to do with that voice is what really counts.

2. A tape recorder.

You will work extensively with this machine, which will give you feedback on your progress. Only by hearing your readings or, "takes," can you learn to analyze and critique your own performance.

3. Ad copy.

This is the material you will be learning to interpret — not just to read — in order to get in touch with its reality. (See the Exercises at the end of this chapter.)

4. A pencil.

In Chapter Three, you will find a system (or you may create your own) of marking copy to help you remember specific emotions or put emphasis on certain words or phrases.

5. A stop watch.

Also in Chapter Three, you will learn how to work with a stop watch to develop an exact sense of timing.

6. A class.

Why bother with a class when you can read a voice-over workbook and learn all the basics? Because a class is the place where you can take risks or "stretch," and get immediate, expert feedback from a professional. Dona Lee Davies feels that a voice-over class is a "must." She encourages students to keep taking classes — from different teachers.

An audition is not the place to try something new. But in a good voice-over class, the environment is supportive. You will be encouraged to explore and develop all dimensions of your voice and learn your strengths and weaknesses. There are other, less tangible, essentials that we feel are equally important.

1. An imagination.

You must be able to visualize yourself as, in order to become, a specific person in a specific situation.

2. A willingness to take/make time to work.

Attending class once a week or skimming through a workbook without ever doing your homework will get you nowhere fast. The pursuit of voice-over excellence requires that you do certain exercises and practice recommended techniques as often as possible — then make time to do them some more.

3. A willingness to play.

Becoming all sorts of different people is exciting if you approach it with the joyful abandon with which children play. Even the most shy child grows bold when he or she "becomes" another person. Remember, it's your game you are playing, so don't waste time being shy with yourself.

Questions:

"What sort of tape recorder do I need?"

One that is easy and comfortable for you to work, which gives you clear playbacks, and which you can reasonably afford. Some people prefer a sophisticated reel-to-reel machine, while others opt for a less expensive cassette player. The cassette recorder is more portable; you can take it to class, for example, to tape guest speakers or your own class work. Neither of us owns a reel-to-reel; we both get along very nicely with cassette players. But some professionals as well as students feel that the quality sound of a reel-to-reel justifies buying one.

"Is there a 'voice-over personality'?"

Most of the people we asked feel that there is definitely a voice-over personality, but it is not easily defined. Here are some of their thoughts.

Nicholas Omana: "The voice-over artist has a profession that is different from a structured, nine-to-five office job. Because of this, voice artists tend to be very disciplined people. They must constantly train, practice, promote themselves and look for work, all on their own. It must also be okay with them to be anonymous. Unless they do on-camera work, even the most famous voice-over artists can walk through a crowd without being recognized. Their egos must consider this a bonus."

Director John Westmoreland: "Voice-over artists can walk into the studio any time, night or day, and always make it seem like ten a.m. (Ten a.m. happens to be a good time of the day for me.) They seem to have a higher metabolism. Also, you don't expect temperament and you don't get it. It is a strange phenomenon that on-camera actors with well-earned reputations for being extremely difficult come in and do voice-overs without one cross word. I don't know why this is true, but it is."

We definitely feel that voice-over actors are unique. They're different from other actors. They are faced with constant opportunities to stretch and grow, and they have to love it. In one day, they may go on more than one audition or job, and be called upon to come up with a number of different characters. Also, the on-camera or stage actor works with only one director, while the voice-over artist may work with several different directors all in the same day.

This takes a special kind of person — flexible, professional, willing to take risks and committed to excellence.

"What are the various types or categories of voice-over spots?"

Ask ten different people involved in voice-overs and they will give you ten different answers.

Voice-overs are usually either commercial or animation. Both categories include singles (one-person spots), doubles (two-person spots) and multiples (more than two people).

Another breakdown, which relates more to the different types of voices that are called for in different spots, includes: straight or "spokes" (spokesperson), commercial character, animation character, promos (promotionals) and informationals (for industrial, educational or religious markets).

"What is the difference between commercial and animation work?"

According to Susan, "Because both involve acting, commercial and animation voice-overs have the same starting point — a slice of life. But whereas commercial voice-overs call for an exaggeration of life within the form of reality, animation voice-overs require an exaggerated exaggeration of life."

Animation work (supplying voices for cartoon characters or inanimate objects) is extremely colorful, and calls for very versatile actors with many different, often far-out character voices. There is absolutely no room for inhibitions in animation work, and its sole purpose is to entertain.

Entertainment is a secondary concern to commercial voice-overs; they must leave the listener remembering the name of the product. Also, commercials are not as vivid as animation voice-overs; they call for subtleties layered over a base of sincerity.

"Do voice-over artists specialize in either animation or commercials?"

Absolutely.

Some voice-over artists prefer animation; others love commercials. It's often a matter of choice. The animation talent enjoys the hyper, off-the-wall animation work and is bored silly by commercials. The commercial talent prefers the more subtle, toned-down approach of commercials, and feels that animation voice artists are usually arrested two-year-olds.

While some voice-over artists can do both, each category requires special skills and abilities.

"Do some voice-over artists specialize in other areas?"

Sure.

Promos, for example. Some voices are more suited to being straight announcer. The artists who can do this work have discovered a strength and are capitalizing on it. Many voice artists prefer this work because it is especially lucrative; by their nature, promos must be constantly changed and updated.

"What about industrials?"

We'll let John Westmoreland, with his extensive background in producing voice-over spots, answer this one.

"Voice-over artists do specialize in the area of industrials or informational films. And I have tremendous respect for these people. They are responsible for doing ten to twenty pages of copy which is filled with technical terms that would make your hair curl. When they are given the copy ahead of time, they look up every single word and come in for a session completely prepared and able to offer alternative pronunciations. They also don't get the multiple takes that regular commercial spots are allowed because there just isn't time, but these people are always economical with our time. Doing voice-overs for the military is even worse, because your access to the copy is often restricted. Talent must go where the copy is being recorded or where it was written, read it there and then record it right away."

"I've done some work as a D.J. Will this help me get into voice-overs?"

Former D.J. Nicholas Omana says: "I learned a lot about the technical aspects of working in a studio while I was a D.J., but that alone did not prepare me to make the transition. D.J.s don't always have the acting ability required to do voice-overs and, frankly, I found the work boring.

"When you are a D.J., you're the same person all the time; with voice-overs, you can be a lot of different people. Doing voice-overs, I have a basic metabolic rate that is twenty percent higher than in any of my other jobs.

Voice-over work is more immediate and it calls for a quick study. Plus, there are a variety of ways to go within your own vocal and attitudinal range."

"I've had acting classes. Isn't that enough?"

No! While acting classes are certainly desirable, there are many techniques and skills that are unique to voice-overs.

Nicholas Omana cautions: "Voice-overs are very personal, much more so than either stage or screen work. As a voice-over artist, you must learn to communicate with your voice. Actors accustomed to on-camera work tend to look up from the copy, either to play to the camera or to get visual feedback from the producer."

"If there are so many voice-over classes around, how do I find out about them and how do I pick the right one for me?"

Voice-over classes are advertised in the trade papers. *Drama-Logue, Daily Variety* and *The Hollywood Reporter* are the most prominent trades circulated in the Los Angeles area. Ask your local magazine store owner for their equivalents in other areas.

The increasing number of voice-over classes indicates that the field is opening up. Dona Lee Davies suggests that before enrolling, you ask the following important questions:

What are the teachers' credits and how do they run their classes?

How large are the classes?

How much mike time are you allowed?

Are there guest speakers (agents, casting directors, other working voice-over professionals, etc.)?

How much do the classes cost?

If possible, arrange an interview with the teacher; choose one whose methods, approach and attitude fit your needs.

Casting director Samantha Paris opened the Voicetrax training center in Sausalito, California, to provide an environment that was completely professional, but also fun and creative—a place where people could feel comfortable exploring their talent and "feel safe even when they fall flat on their face," she says. "Success in voice-over isn't some God-given talent that some people have and others don't. In my heart, I believe that anyone with a desire to do voice-over has the potential to succeed as a voice-over actor. However, it requires a willingness to risk your emotions, and the confidence to make a choice and commit to it. It also depends upon a willingness to study, practice, and face down your own fears as you let down the barriers between you and your emotions. Finally, you must develop the discipline to call upon those emotions and apply them with skill. That's hard work!"

Exercises:

Loosening-up Exercises.

These exercises are designed to relieve tension, to relax neck, face and mouth muscles, and to open up the vocal range. They should be done while standing up, although most may be modified for use while sitting down. Consult your physician to make sure these exercises are for you, or ask the doctor to provide substitute exercises which will accomplish the same things. Never force your efforts past your level of tolerance, and stop immediately if you experience any pain.

A. Inhale deeply through the nose, then exhale slowly through the mouth.

Do this three times.

B. Inhale slowly and deeply through the nose, filling the lungs to ninety-percent capacity. Feel the diaphragm being pushed out. Quickly inhale the last ten percent of air into the lungs and then let the breath out slowly, vocalizing an extended *"ahhhh"* sound during the entire exhalation.

Repeat once or twice.

C. Slowly, and without jerky movements, touch your left ear to your left shoulder, right ear to your right shoulder.

Repeat several times.

D. Drop your chin to your chest, then roll your head around in a loose, slow, 360-degree turn.

Reverse the direction of the roll and repeat.

E. Like a dog shaking its fur, shake your body from your shoulders on down.

F. From the diaphragm, repeat *"Huh! Huh! Huh! Huh!"* in short, powerful bursts.

G. Using the sound *"ee,"* bring your voice from its highest to its lowest pitch in a slow, sliding descent. Start by placing the voice in the very top of your head, then (slowly) bring it down into your forehead, nose, mouth, throat, chest, stomach, legs, down through your feet and out your toes.

Using the same *"ee"* sound, take the voice from its lowest to its highest pitch in a slow, sliding ascent. Make sure the voice is placed in the appropriate part of the body each step of the way and you will open up all your vocal areas. Repeat this exercise, using all the vowel sounds.

H. Make like a racing car engine (*"Brrrrrr!"*) and expel air through your lips. Do this several times. The vibrations will help to keep your lips loose and relaxed.

I. Pronounce the words *"good blood, bad blood"* very slowly, greatly exaggerating every sound. Keep your lips broad and loose. Say the words over and over, gradually increasing speed without losing clarity of diction.

Repeat this exercise, using the words *"red leather, yellow leather," "guttah, buttah,"* and *"buttah, guttah."* This will help you warm up your mouth and ready your instrument for play.

Begin collecting ad copy.

Go through magazines and select ads with copy that appeals to you. We all have a picture of the image we project, so go ahead and choose copy that you can easily and naturally see yourself doing. (We have provided some original copy at the end of this chapter.)

At this point, we would recommend that you not use copy you have written. Being too familiar with the copy can hinder your ability to read copy written by other people, which is what you will be doing on an audition or job.

Get to know your voice.

Select a piece of ad copy and tape several readings of it without trying to change your natural voice in any way. Don't listen to your voice while you are recording — that's what playbacks are for.

Now play back your takes and make notes. Pretend you've never heard that voice before. Your assignment is to describe it in five words to someone whose only experience with the voice will be your description of it. Forget your lack of training for the moment — don't critique the reading — just determine what strikes you about that voice. What qualities would identify it to another person?

Also, listen for words you have difficulty pronouncing and work on them. You never know when they'll catch up with you. "I'd always had trouble saying the word *aluminum*," says Susan, "but I just ignored it. One day I auditioned for a job which would have meant a lot of money. I hadn't bothered to ask my agent what the product was. Naturally, the spot was all about aluminum, and I just couldn't get that word out of my mouth. I'd been careless and unprofessional, and now I was terribly embarrassed! I went straight home, determined to stay there until I could say *aluminum* correctly."

Knowing what you do best is only the starting point. We want to enhance your natural voice with a few professional tips, then help you discover all the other people (voices) who are inside you, waiting for their turn at the mike. Here's the copy we promised you. Throughout the book and on the audio cassette tape that is also available, we have written commercials using the names of products and companies which, to the best of our knowledge, are all fictitious. If any of our work contains existing copy, or the names of actual products or companies, our use of them was unintentional and coincidental.

The first spot is as much an exercise as it is ad copy. All it needs at the end is a tag (such as "Crowley's Health Insurance — we care about you all along the way."), and it would be a true commercial.

By using this piece of copy as a guide, improvise with your own imagined thoughts and feelings at these stages of life. You will learn what ages you do easily and well. Remember to get into each section by having a certain person in mind and becoming that person. Don't get discouraged if you can't do each age perfectly. This is a tough spot, and even the best have difficulty with it.

> (Infant crying ... to "goo's" ... to
> laughing.)
>
> I'm three years old and I love my Mommy
> and Daddy and I like to ride my tricycle
> and I like to feel the wind on my face
> and to splash in puddles after it rains,
> but Mommy says that's how you catch a
> cold.
>
> Now I'm six and I'm getting dressed for
> my first day of school, but I wanna know
> how come I can't take my puppy with me?
> He's going to be all alone and I'm gonna
> miss him...
>
> You see, I'm ten years old and I ride my
> bike to school and you can't come with us

'cause you're just a peewee. (Laugh).
Come on, you guys, let's get going!

Well, I'm thirteen and I just won this
spelling bee. Do you think that cute boy
(girl) noticed me up there on stage? I
think maybe I'll see if he (she) wants to
go out with me.

I'm seventeen years old and I'm going off
to college pretty soon. I'm real excited
about living on campus in a dorm — but I
know I'm gonna miss my family and friends
back home. I'm going for a Liberal Arts
degree and then...who knows? What I really want to do is write — be a great nov-
elist.

Well, I'm twenty-five now and I'm working
for the town newspaper. I just wish I had
more exciting assignments than interviewing the winner of a local chili cook-off.
I'm hoping to land a job with a big metro-
politan paper and cover real news!

I turned forty last week. It's hard to believe time can pass so quickly. I'm edi-
tor of my old hometown newspaper now and
I feel like I've found the work I want to
do for the rest of my career. I've made
some big changes here...The old Tribune
is now a vital, dynamic force in this community — and I've boosted advertising rev-
enues 50%.

So, I retired last week at the ripe old
age of sixty. My kids have grown up now
and have their own families. They come to

visit us on holidays and I stuff myself
so full of food (laugh), it just about
fills me up till they visit next time. I
guess now's the time to write that
novel...

My, my, I turned seventy-five last month.
The great-grandchildren bought me this
fine rocking chair. I guess they think
I've got nothing better to do than sit up
here on this creaky old porch thinking
about the old days. Well, I'm on my third
novel now and this one's about...

Looking back, I figure I did most of what
I set out to do — though lots of times
along the way I wondered where life was
taking me. If I can give you just one bit
of advice: Live life to the fullest every
moment of every day, and don't forget to
stop and smell the flowers.

LANDER'S LONG DISTANCE DIALING

Hello, Paul? How's college? ... This is
your mother — the one who did your laundry for the past eighteen years. ...
Right, that one. You never call me. ... I
know you moved out only two days ago. Two
whole days and you never called me! ...
'Expensive'? Not if you have Lander's.
... Lander's Long Distance Dialing. ...
That's the phone system your father put
in so you could call all your long-distance girlfriends for practically nothing, remember? ... Right, that one. Get
Lander's, Paul, and call your mother once

in a blue moon. ... Lander's. How do you
think we could afford to send you to college?

CREAHAN'S COMPUTER DATING

I thought computer dating was for the
much younger crowd. But then my daughter
Caroline talked me into signing up. Am I
ever glad she did! That's how I met Pete
(Cathy). He's (she's) wonderful and we
have so much in common. Now Pete (Cathy)
and I are going to talk my daughter into
signing up. After all, three is a crowd.

CALDE'S CREAMY LIP GLOSS

(Note: "Calde" is pronounced "caldee,"
with the accent on the first syllable.)

When my baby puts on Calde's Creamy Lip
Gloss, I can't resist kissing those perfectly beautiful lips ... which means she
has to put on more Calde's Creamy Lip
Gloss ... which means I have to kiss her
again ... which means more Calde's Creamy
Lip Gloss ... which means another kiss
... which means ... another perfectly
beautiful evening!

NUTS

Nuts — the fun food. Now that nut prices
are down, buy them in quantity. And turn
your home into a real nut house.

"SHANNON'S BANDAGES"

Oh boy, am I in trouble! Wait'll Mom sees
my knees. I didn't mean to fall out of
that tree. But I saw those birds and they
were building a nest and I wanted to see
it up close. I didn't know the branch was
gonna break. Maybe Mom'll put that sting-
ing stuff on my knees. I don't like that
at all. But I do like what she puts on
after. They're called "Shannon's Bandages." They're pretty and they make me
feel good. (CALLING) Hey, Mom, do we have
any Shannon's Bandages? I wanna feel good!

DONNA'S TRAVEL AGENCY

I love to travel. And I do a lot of it.
Mostly for business. But when I'm not on
a business trip, I travel for fun. And
whether my trip is for work or play, I
let Donna's Travel Agency make all my res-
ervations. Their service is terrific.
Sure I could do it myself, but I deserve
the best. I call Donna's Travel Agency.

MARG'S DINER

When I get the hungries, I head over to
Marg's. It's this great little diner just
down the road, and Marg herself does all
the cooking. You just can't beat Marg's
lamb curry or her pork chops, and her

Yorkshire pudding is something to write home about. Even if your Mom lives in England! So come on down to Marg's and treat yourself to some real good eating.

BOOKKEEPING BY JANE

When I started designing men's clothes, I did all my own accounting. But when the business really took off, I let all that bookkeeping stuff slide. Then the I.R.S. came in and wanted to know what I'd been doing. "Creating," I told them. "Not good enough," they told me. So I got an accountant. Jane's her name and she comes in once a week to do my bookkeeping. Now my records are accurate to the penny, thanks to Jane. If you're honestly too busy "creating" to get to the books, call Jane. She'll keep you honest.

PARTIES BY NANCY

Want to give a special party and you don't know what to do? Nancy does. She's an expert when it comes to planning and organizing parties. For two or two hundred, Nancy knows exactly what to do to make your party very special. Just give her the date, time and place, and she'll do the rest — from addressing and sending out your invitations, to planning the menu and hiring the caterers. Nancy. She knows how to make your party special because she's special.

Chapter Two

The Basic Process

What we call The Basic Process is the foundation of voice-over excellence. If you read no other Chapter, read—and remember—this one.

Larry Belling, who writes and produces radio commercials for such clients as American Express and all the major motion picture studios at his own Slippery Studios in Hollywood, says: "The most successful voice-over talents share five common attributes: They have an original style of reading copy, subtlety of delivery, a voice that commands attention, a consistency in their read and, most important, an instant comprehension of what the commercial's writer wants to convey to the listening audience."

The best voice-overs are the ones that the consumers find most believable. Your listeners will not act on your recommendations unless they trust your voice. They will believe what you are saying only if you believe it. But in order for you to believe it, you must first know what is happening in the copy.

Ad copy is more than just a bunch of words strung together to promote a product. It is very much like a miniature play, with a beginning, a middle and an end. One or more characters are involved, and it takes place at a particular time and place. You need to discover all those elements and more to act out the copy.

Samantha Paris says, "Good voice-over requires committing so thoroughly to a character that the listener gets caught up in your world. Sometimes you have only 30 seconds to create an entire world." How do you get in touch with the reality of the copy? By using our Basic Process which works every time: Focus, Visualize, and Commit.

1. Focus your energy on doing the voice-over.

Minimize and/or eliminate all distractions. Unplug the telephone or turn on the answering machine; cover the chattering cockatoo's cage; ignore your unvacuumed, undusted surroundings and the growing pile of laundry in the corner. Concentrate all your energy on the voice-over work in front of you.

2. Visualize the copy.

Ask yourself certain questions about it. Sometimes the answers will be obvious; sometimes you will have to invent them. If you don't feel comfortable with an obvious answer, substitute one that works for you. Be specific in your choices and draw on your own experiences.

Select a piece of copy and go through the process with it, step-by-step. Move slowly and deliberately the first time so that the learning really sinks in. With practice, you'll pick up speed and proficiency.

Answer the following questions about the copy and do the process as directed:

A. Who is speaking?

Who are you — a mother, father, daughter, son, teacher, next-door neighbor, etc.? Remember to be very specific in your choice; don't just be a teacher, be a particular teacher. "Go inside and find one" (i.e., think back and pull a suitable one out of your memory or, later, out of your repertory of characters), and become that person.

How? Just as if you were getting dressed: Have a clear and detailed picture of the person in your mind, and then — item by item — put on his or her name, age, face, characteristics, mannerisms, clothes and, especially, attitude.

Don't bypass this process and just try to imitate the voice. You will get bogged down in the concept of how it sounds — the result — and you'll start criticizing yourself while trying to do the voice. When that happens, you will lose that wonderful character you've created, as well as your potential for an excellent reading. If you successfully become everything else about a character, his or her voice will automatically come out of that process.

To whom are you speaking? Your aunt, your boss, your lover, etc.? Get a clear picture of the particular person for whom your words are meant. If you really talk to this person, you will automatically be talking to all your listeners. But the minute you lose this one person and address all your listeners, you will automatically sound like an impersonal announcer.

Make a choice (determine who you are and to whom you are speaking) and then tape the copy. Don't play it back now, but make another choice and tape the copy again. Repeat this process several times and then play back your takes. Notice how your voice changes as your choices change — as you become different people.

B. What is happening?

We don't talk to other people in a vacuum. Other things are going on at the same time. Are you washing dishes while the other person dries them? Having a last-minute conversation with your spouse while he/she is getting ready to go out jogging? Driving to work and talking things over with a member of your car pool?

Once you decide what is happening, you must also ask "What is the pre-life?" Pre-life refers to what was going on with your character just before he or she starts to speak.

Were you out on a much-needed coffee break? Did your favorite team just win the pennant? Were you having dinner at a special restaurant?

You probably won't find this information spelled out in the copy, but the commercial itself may suggest what was happening and your imagination must take it from there. Having a pre-life in mind will help you avoid cold, abrupt beginnings to your readings.

Now, make a choice as to who you are and to whom you are speaking, and also decide what is going on during and just prior (pre-life) to your take. Tape the copy using these choices and notice in playback how another interesting layer has been added to your readings.

C. When is this sales pitch taking place?

Is it an "early morning spot" which would call for a bright and cheerful delivery? Or does it take place late in the evening when a more laid-back approach would be appropriate?

Do it as several different people talking to different people at various times of the day, choosing a specific pre-life and action for each take. Notice how much richer your readings are becoming as more dimensions are added.

D. Where is this happening?

Are you at a loud party where you would have to raise your voice to be heard? Are you at home where you can occasionally lower your voice and still make a point? Are you in a park where you are competing only with the sounds of Nature?

Be in various places and do several takes as different individuals talking to a variety of listeners at certain times of the day and, of course, select a specific pre-life and concurrent action for each take. In playback, see how yet another layer has been added to your performance.

E. Why am I doing this?

Whatever personal reasons you may have for doing voice-overs, you are really reading the copy to sell a product — the "newest," "fastest," "safest," "softest." But superseding all the adjectives is your belief — without reservation — that this product is the very best one there is. You know it; you just want someone else to know it, too.

Do several more tapings, experimenting with different choices as to who, what, when, where, and be very aware of the product and of its excellence. Play back the takes and notice how the name and the qualities of the product stand out — you have automatically (by staying in the process and out of the result) highlighted them.

3. Commit to your answers to the above questions.

Once you have made your choices, stick to them throughout the entire taping. You can always go back and do it again another way. The sharper and clearer your picture of the copy, the sharper and clearer your reading will be — and the sharper and clearer your listeners' picture will be, too.

If you don't fully commit to all your answers, your readings will reflect this uncertainty and lack of conviction. And you will lose the trust of your listeners.

Now, rewind your tape completely and play back all your takes. Notice again how they become richer and more interesting as more dimensions are layered into your readings. The copy really comes alive, doesn't it? Voice-over artist Brian Cummings says you must "build the copy into a living human being." He reads the copy, determines its message, and then gets a human relationship going. He emphasizes that a voice-over can't be just aural; in order for it to work, it must also be visual. After all, if you can't picture the person to whom you are speaking, how can you expect anyone else to?

Brian also advises us to remember that the person to whom we are speaking will have his or her own set of changing reactions — ranging from hostile skepticism to outright acceptance. While doing a reading, "see" that person's particular reaction at any given moment and your delivery will vary accordingly.

The Basic Process will never let you down. Using it allows you to make the copy your own little drama or comedy with its own life and vitality. Susan calls it "endowing the copy" — with that which makes it special or unique to you. And then your listeners will feel that it's special to them, too.

Questions

"What if the person speaking is a person I don't have inside me?"

If you can't find a particular person inside you, substitute someone else who can feel the same way about the product and about what is happening in the copy. Become that person and let him or her speak. This is a fail-safe technique that will always get you past this dilemma.

"This copy is supposed to take place on a farm. I've never set foot on one. What should I do?"

Again, use substitution. Determine whether your copy is a comfortable soft sell (most likely true for a farm setting) or a more driving hard sell. If soft (also called "a passive commercial"), picture yourself in your favorite quiet spot — the beach, a mountain cabin — wherever your special place is. Your delivery will take on a calm, relaxed quality that suggests rural peace.

If the copy is a hard sell (also called an "active commercial"), imagine yourself in the board room of a Fortune 500 company, addressing a group of tough business executives, and your delivery will be charged with believable electricity.

"I can't always figure out who the other person is."

Rather than addressing yourself to a vague, general audience, pick a particular relative or friend with whom a conversation always brings up a similar reaction. For example, Molly Ann's father has an incurable sweet tooth. When stuck for that "other person" to whom she must soft sell something sweet, she always substitutes her Dad.

On one audition Susan went through her entire repertory of friends and relatives and could not come up with the other person. Instead of giving up, she visualized a man — just an ordinary, all-American, middle-income guy — driving along in his car, listening to her voice on the radio, and spoke directly to him.

We recommend this technique only as a last resort. You use more energy "making up" a person than picturing one whom you know well and who is easy to visualize.

"I've gone over this copy ten times and I still can't get a handle on it. Should I just keep on reading it over and over?"

At this point, we doubt if even reading it fifty more times will give you the answers.You will also be under a time constraint in an audition or a job; you won't have the luxury of unlimited hours to study the text.

Slippery Studios' Larry Belling advises: "Here's a trick used by many voices. When they first look at a script, they read the last lines first. The last lines in the copy usually tell exactly what the writer is trying to say. This sets the tone and attitude for the entire reading of the spot."

That's good advice. Try reading the copy line by line from the bottom up. When you see where you are going, you'll have a clearer idea of how to get there. With this technique you'll know the end or highpoint of the text so you won't start your reading too high (at the same emotional level you would like to hit for the ending) and leave yourself nowhere to go with it.

Also try reading the copy a sentence or phrase at a time, and keep asking "what" or "why" for everything you read. Here's an example of what we mean. First, the text:

```
          I could never understand why my
          brother liked cottage cheese.
          It's always so runny and lumpy.
          Then he told me his secret: He
          buys Mullin's Small Curd Cot-
          tage Cheese. So I went out and
          bought some. And you know what?
          It's great — real smooth and
          creamy — the way cottage cheese
          should be. Mullin's Small Curd
          Cottage Cheese — it's the best!
```

Now, let's tear the text apart by asking "what" or "why."

What are the first few words of the copy? *"I could never understand ..."*

You were confused about something. What couldn't you understand? *"... why my brother liked cottage cheese."*

He liked cottage cheese; you didn't. Why not? Because it was *"... always so runny and lumpy."*

If the cottage cheese you've tried is always runny and lumpy, why would anyone in his right mind — even your brother — buy some? It's *"... his secret ..."* Ah hah! What is his secret? *"... Mullin's Small Curd Cottage Cheese."*

What's so special about Mullin's Small Curd Cottage Cheese? *"It's great ..."*

Why is it great? Because it's *"... real smooth and creamy—the way cottage cheese should be."*

You've finally found the answer to your cottage cheese problems. What is the name of that wonderful product again?

"Mullin's Small Curd Cottage Cheese ..."

Why "Mullin's"? Because *"... it's the best!"*

This quickie what/why process will begin to give you some clues to the emotions and action that are taking place in the copy. But it is only a beginning. Once you have a handle on what is going on (and why), you still need to bring the scenario to life using the Basic Process.

Exercises:

Practice and practice and practice the Basic Process until it becomes second nature to you. Don't even think about going on to the next Chapter until you have learned this technique. Other techniques and refinements you will pick up later. Right now, mastering the Basic Process is your priority. Without it, all your readings will sound alike — and that sound will be mechanical and lacking in conviction. Only by internalizing the Basic Process will you be able to instinctively and naturally give the most believable readings.

When listening to your work, practice being objective about that process. Do not judge. Your attention will be on the last reading and will leave no room for the next. "That was a terrible reading!" is a negative judgment.

"I didn't have a clear picture of who was speaking" is a constructive criticism. Constructive criticism has a positive, built-in indicator of what you need to do to make your reading better. In this case, the indicator tells you: "I need to have a clearer picture of who I am."

Practice not listening to your voice while you are taping. Forget the picture of Gary Owens, hand cupped to his ear, delivering his wonderfully zany messages on LAUGH-IN. Gary was always and intentionally the "Announcer;" that was his character. But your characters are meant to be real people, and real people don't talk like that.

You can always tell when someone is listening to his or her own voice. Whatever picture that person started out with is lost as he or she focuses on the results (the sound). Consequently, the listeners' picture is also lost as the reading loses its internal life and falls flat.

Listen to radio and television voice-overs. Decide which ones you like and which you dislike — and then figure out why you liked or disliked each one. Notice how a spot works because you can clearly see what the speaker is picturing. Also, notice how often the reasons a spot doesn't work tie in to factors you learned in the Basic Process. Remember, when you hear a line reading you particularly like, don't try to duplicate it. Identify the quality or attitude you like about it and learn to duplicate that. It is that attitude — and not the line reading itself — that can be adapted to any copy, and can go with you on any audition or job.

Turn the sound completely off when you watch a commercial on television. Do all the voices (be all the characters) in that spot. Record your voice and videotape the spot as well, if you have the equipment to do so. In playback, see if you were able to capture the various qualities and moods of the pictures.

Try writing your own commercial. Start with a product you like and then build a text using the questions in the Basic Process to flesh out the scenario. Remember to give it a beginning, a middle and an end. Keep it "tight." Don't use unnecessary words. Feature the name of the product and its selling points, and make it sincere and convincing. Either you will find you have a knack for writing ad copy (in which case you may want to write some material for your demo tape — see Chapter Seven), or you will begin to feel that crawling on your knees over cut glass is a lot more fun than writing copy. In that case you will be left with a healthy respect for the few good copywriters there are; they elevate the form to an art.

Chapter Three

Refinements

In this Chapter we'll polish your developing skills as we take a look at some of the more technical aspects of doing voice-overs.

Notice how people naturally speak. Their conversations are filled with sounds such as *um's, oh's, uh's,* etc. If you can add some of these to your readings, without having them sound forced or strained, your performance will seem even more relaxed and natural.

For example, tape the line *"This is delicious!"* just as it's written. Now tape it this way: *"Mmmm, this is delicious!"* Hear the difference? The line becomes more interesting and begins to acquire a personality of its own.

Stress and Emphasis

In reading over your copy, you will need to stress or emphasize particular words to get the meaning across. Pat Fraley, one of the busiest and most talented voice-over artists around, suggests four different means by which you may stress or emphasize a word: loudness, pitch, duration and pauses.

1. An increase or decrease in loudness.

This has to do with volume only. Keeping your voice in a monotone, tape the phrase *I love you,* emphasizing the word *I.* Next tape the phrase, stressing the word *love.* Finally, tape the line and hit the word *you.*

Play back the takes and notice how increasing the volume of the word *I* gives the phrase the meaning: *They* may not love you, but *I* do. Emphasizing the word *love* makes that verb-action very important and special: I don't just *like* you; *I love* you. When you emphasize the word *you*, a third meaning becomes apparent: *I don't love someone else; I love you.*

Repeat the exercise, using the phrase *They're here*, and this time decrease the volume of each word. Remember to keep it all monotone. In playback, hear how the readings differ in meaning. In one, a decrease in volume can indicate awe or fear as to who is here; in the other, location becomes important as we sense that they are very close.

As you go through these exercises, remember that one reading is not necessarily right or better than another. Our purpose is simply to let you experience how different readings may be obtained by using different techniques.

2. Raising or lowering the pitch.

Pitch has to do with the musical level at which we speak, the up's and down's our voices take in normal conversation. First, for contrast, tape the phrase *For me?* in a monotone, without increasing or decreasing the volume of either word. Tape it again, this time letting your voice go up in pitch on the word *me*. Hear how the second take says more clearly: *Gee, out of all the other people it could be for, is it really for me?*

Tape the phrase *I'm sad* in a monotone. Now tape it and let your voice register lower on the scale on *sad*, without prolonging the word itself. In playback, hear how much sadder your second take sounds.

Tape the phrase *That's the strangest thing I've ever seen* in a monotone. Now tape it letting your voice go up and down in pitch (not volume) wherever it feels right. Chances are your inflections fell on the words *strangest* and *ever*. Try it again, hitting *that's, thing, I've* and *seen*, and then try emphasizing various combinations of those words. Hear how the different emphases result in slightly different readings.

Raising and lowering your pitch is a great way to emphasize words in a long sentence that's packed with adjectives. You'll come across many of these since advertisers love to extol each and every virtue, real or imagined, of their products. These long strings of words are called "laundry lists."

Tape the sentence *Now these are brownies — fresh-baked, oven-warm, moist and chewy, and so chocolatey!* Let your voice go up in pitch from one word to the next. Notice the excitement building in the reading as each word becomes more important and more appealing than the last.

3. Prolonging or shortening the duration of a syllable, word or phrase.

Tape the phrase *I'm hungry* in a monotone. Now tape it, prolonging the first syllable of the word *hungry*. Hear how much hungrier you are in the second take.

Tape the phrase *I'm scared*. Then tape it, prolonging the word *scared*. Hear how much more frightened you sound in the second take.

Tape the sentence *It costs only one dollar and that's all*. Next tape it prolonging the phrase *It costs only one dollar*. Retape it, prolonging the phrase *and that's all*. Notice how the second take calls attention to the amount of money it costs, while the third take emphasizes how small that amount really is.

Tape the phrase *He's uptight*. Now tape it, shortening the second syllable of *uptight*. Hear how much more uptight he is in the second take.

Tape the phrase *You're right*. Now tape it, shortening the word *right*. The second reading may sound a bit stilted, almost as if you resented the other person's being right.

Finally, tape the sentence *We can't go in there — it's off limits*. Next tape it, shortening the phrase *We can't go in there*. Then tape it, shortening the phrase *it's off limits*. The second take sounds as if you were in a hurry to warn someone not to go in there. The third take calls attention to why you can't go in there — because it's off limits.

4. Pausing before, during, or after a syllable, word or phrase.

In normal speech, people often hesitate between words, phrases and even syllables. A pause can be a powerful and dramatic addition to your reading, but first a word of caution: A voice-over pause must never be as long as a regular pause or your reading will sound as if it died. A voice-over pause automatically seems twice as long as a regular pause simply because there is usually nothing else going on at that moment to fill in the gap and hold your listeners' attention. All they hear is a lot of dead air.

With that in mind, tape the phrase *Believe it!* as written. In the second taping, pause (briefly!) between the two syllables in *believe*. You'll hear how much more you want your listener to believe it.

Tape the phrase *I love you*. Retape it with a pause between the words *I* and *love*. Notice how much more emotion the second take has.

Tape the sentence *She used to work here, but that was a long time ago.* Now tape it, pausing between the two phrases. The second take comes across with more nostalgia.

Pat cautions that on an audition or a job you will not have a lot of time to determine how each syllable, word or phrase is to be read. Nor should that be your primary concern. Pat recommends that you first look at the emotional life of a line and then make a choice as to how you would like to read it.

And how do you determine what that emotional life is? By understanding what is going on in the copy — which brings us right back to the Basic Process.

A quick way to find natural stress points in copy is by doing another type of *what* exercise. Read the copy aloud, phrase by phrase, in character, and after each phrase ask yourself *what?* This *what* is not the *what did you mean?* of Chapter Two's what/why exercise, but simply a *what did you say?* as in: *Excuse me, I didn't quite hear what you said.* When your character then repeats each phrase, you will find yourself listening more closely to the copy and automatically stressing certain parts of it quite naturally.

When you have answered the Basic Process questions and made some choices concerning stress or emphasis for a particular reading, it is most helpful to have a system of marking the copy to remind you of those choices. Also, you may be given quite a bit of direction on a job and you need a quick way of noting those changes on your copy.

We will share our own copy-marking system with you, but we do so somewhat reluctantly. On the theory that you retain more easily that which you yourself create, we strongly recommend that you develop your own system. Use our notations only if you can't come up with your own symbols or if you feel perfectly comfortable with ours.

We have not developed a corresponding symbol for every technique of stress or emphasis that we discussed earlier. We have found that the following symbols have adequately met all our needs in marking copy. Should you wish to expand on our system, feel free to do so.

To indicate that a word or phrase is to be read more loudly, we draw a straight line under it:

I love you.

These cookies are great — did you make them?

To raise the pitch of a word or phrase, draw an arrow which points upward over it:

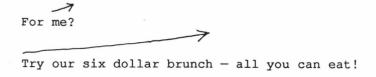

For me?

Try our six dollar brunch — all you can eat!

To lower the pitch of a word or phrase, draw an arrow pointing downward over it:

I'm sad.

Come to New Zealand — enjoy quiet beauty.

In the sentence *That's the strangest thing I've ever seen,* suppose we wanted to put some inflection into the words *strangest* and *ever.* We would mark the words:

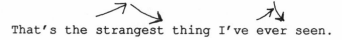

That's the strangest thing I've ever seen.

To indicate a pause before, during, or after a syllable, word or phrase, we use one downstroke line to indicate the break:

Be⎮lieve it.

I ⎮ love you.

She used to work here,⎮ but that was a long time ago.

The punctuation that is marked on a piece of copy is not necessarily the punctuation you have to follow. More interesting and natural readings often occur when you ignore the given punctuation (or lack thereof) and pencil in your own. We sprinkle question marks and exclamation points liberally throughout copy, and we use parentheses to indicate word groupings we would like to make in our readings. Suppose a line is written:

```
My interview was in ten minutes and my clothes were
all wrinkled.
```

We would mark and read it:

(My interview was in ten minutes!)(and my clothes were all wrinkled !!!!)

Our symbols for emotions are capital letters with circles drawn around them. We recommend that you mark emotions only when they go against the way a line would normally be read. For example, the line *I hate you!* would ordinarily be read with anger. In this case, there is no need to mark what is implicit in the line.

But suppose you are directed to read that same line as if you were afraid (i.e., against the text). We would put our symbol for afraid (AF), slightly above and to the left of the line in question:

```
I hate you.
```

If an entire section is to be read against the text, we put a larger version of the symbol notation for the emotion in the margin next to the section.

We use the following signs to indicate some of the ways copy may be read. Before adopting our symbols, try developing your own. They'll feel more natural to you and come to mind more easily.

(LO) - loving   (AN) - angry

(LI) - light   (AF) - afraid

(TH) - threatening   (HA) - happy

(SX) - sexy   (HV) - heavy

(SD) - sad   (WR) - worried

Now let's mark an entire piece of copy. First, take a look at the raw text:

When it comes to diets, I'm an expert.
There isn't one I haven't tried. But nothing ever worked for me until I discovered
Diet Dinners. New Diet Frozen Dinners satisfied my cravings for sinfully delicious
meals and with so few calories, I
couldn't help but lose weight. If you'd
like to shed a few pounds painlessly, try
Diet Dinners. The tasteful way to a slim-
mer you.

Here's the text as we would mark it for a reading:

When it comes to _diets_, I'm an expert.
There _isn't_ _one_ I haven't tried. But
nothing ever worked for me _until_ I discovered _Diet_ _Dinners!_ New Diet Frozen Dinners satisfied my cravings for sinfully
delicious meals and with _so_ _few_ _calories_,
I couldn't help but _lose_ _weight!_ If you'd
like to shed a few pounds painlessly, try
Diet Dinners. The tasteful way to a _slim-_
mer _you!_

Most copy should be delivered with a smile on your lips. Tape a piece of copy with and without a smile. Hear how much warmer the smile makes the copy. Even when the tone of the copy is serious, you can let that concern come through in your reading, but generally at some point there is room for a hopeful, problem-solving moment.

When Susan did a commercial for a medical pain center, she was directed to keep the tone serious and subdued, which she did. Yet at the end she let a little smile warm up the copy since the final message was one of hope: *Relief is available.*

A good way to keep your delivery fresh is to add the element of surprise to your performance. Discover something new each time you go through the copy, and read it as if you were pleasantly surprised to learn about that particular feature of the product. Your discovery becomes your listeners' discovery, and the attraction the product holds for you becomes theirs — which means they'll probably buy the product the next time they go shopping.

Another way to keep your readings fresh is to leave the chronological age of a character alone, but change his or her energy age. If your character is a seventy-year-old grandparent, for example, stay seventy but think twenty.

Your listeners will hear a seventy-year-old speaking, but as if this was the first time he or she ever spoke those words.

Never let the end of a spot drop — which it will if you allow your voice to go down in volume or energy. Even if you feel that the last line should just comfortably fade away, punch it up anyway. It is the last thing your listeners hear, and it often contains the most important information about a product or the product's name itself. This especially applies to a soft sell where you're holding your audience by a loose thread which can break very easily. Your loss of intensity means their loss of interest. Always go for a strong finish to make a lasting impression on your listeners.

When delivering copy, use your hands and body freely to become a particular character and to act out the play. If your character has a bad leg, for example, favor that leg at the mike. If your character has a habit of shaking his or her finger to make a point, do so.

Just don't hit the mike! And don't turn your head away from the mike unless you are specifically directed to or you do so intentionally as a technique.

Also, if you are working a mike with one or more other people, courtesy and concern for their safety oblige you to confine your gestures and movements.

"I learned the hard way," says Molly Ann. "I was auditioning for a double and my partner was standing to my left. The spot was for an exciting get-away trip to a fun-filled island with wide, sweeping beaches and ... you guessed it. When I hit 'wide, sweeping beaches,' I also hit my partner in the stomach. Actually, he took it quite well. Once he stopped gasping for air, he gently suggested that 'those wide, sweeping beaches might just as easily sweep off to the right, mightn't they?'"

Practice using a script stand for your copy. Adjustable music stands are excellent for this purpose. Holding the script in your hands is very unprofessional, and you will get paper noise as you record.

Headphones are fun to work with and you might want to spend some time getting used to them, but they are rarely used on an audition or job unless you are working with music.

Let's talk about Mike Technique. On an audition or job, the mike will often be your best and only friend. Practice getting so comfortable with the following techniques that you can simply relax and "romance" the mike when you do a reading.

1. In a class situation, you may be allowed to adjust the mike to your own height. If so, mike courtesy calls for you to tighten the adjustment only to the point where the next person can loosen it with just two fingers.

On a job or an audition, never touch any of the equipment unless you are specifically asked to do so. And you won't be, unless it's a nonunion house.

2. Consistency. Unless your vocal highs and lows change drastically, always stay the same distance away from the mike. Twelve to fourteen inches is recommended for a normal speaking voice.

The engineer must be able to pull a line from one of your earlier takes and cut it into copy from a later reading.

A. If you are using a Lavalier mike, make sure your script is angled low enough so that sound will not reflect off the script and into the mike. This will cause phase interference.

WRONG   RIGHT

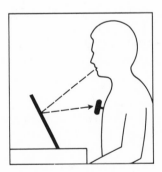
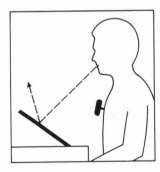

B. If you are using the more standard cardioid mike, again position your script (usually to one side of the mike) so your sound will reflect off the script or script stand and away from the microphone.

WRONG   RIGHT

   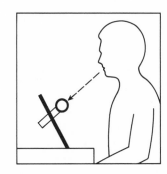

3. For more intimate copy, move in closer to the mike and speak more softly. Softly does not mean a soundless whisper; there must be some sound or your voice will not be picked up. Experiment to see how much and how little sound you can get away with at various distances from the mike.

4. If you are going to read a part of your copy very loudly, always tell the engineer in advance. Unless adjustments are made, equipment can be damaged.

When increasing the volume on a line, take one or two steps back from the mike, deliver the line (without turning your head away from the mike), then move back in to your original position. You can also stay at the mike, but turn your head away to deliver a loud line, then turn back to the mike. Remember to do these movements quickly and not while you are speaking, or you will get sloppy fade-out/fade-in effects as your other lines are delivered at various distances from the mike.

Treat the mike as you would the ear of a good friend. You wouldn't shout into your friend's ear; you might injure it. On the other hand, more intimate copy just begs to be whispered in someone special's ear, so move on in and share it with your friend.

5. Pop filters are styrofoam balls that fit over the mike and reduce the chances of Ps and other hard consonants being popped. At home, you can make a pop filter by stretching nylon panty hose over a coat hanger or by putting a sock over the mike. If *Ps, Bs, Ts,* etc. are still problems, when you come to one of these letters, quickly duck your head down or to one side of the mike to say the letter and then quickly raise your head back to the mike. This requires practice, but the clean takes you will get are worth the effort.

6. Never blow into a mike. This can do a great deal of damage to the equipment. It is the telltale mark of a nonprofessional.

7. Mouth noises. A dry mouth can come from spending a lot of time at the mike or it can be the result of a bad case of nerves. Either way, it produces clicking noises when you record. Keep some water handy to wet your whistle as needed. Also, just before you speak, hold your mouth in an open position so you won't get a beginning click on your takes.

8. Mikes are very sensitive, so watch what you wear when you are recording at home, in class and, especially, when you go on an audition or a job. Beeping watches, jangling jewelry, loose change, keys clipped onto belts, materials that rustle (nylon pants or jackets) — anything that makes a noise (other than your mouth) — should either be left at home or kept well out of mike range.

A very famous rock star was in a recording session not long ago and his engineer was going crazy trying to locate the source of a faint but persistant noise that plagued every take. The rock star did not appear to be wearing or carrying anything that could cause a problem, so the engineer decided it had to be in his soundboard.

He tried everything until finally, in desperation, he tore his board apart to look for the noise. He had done thousands of dollars' worth of looking, before someone discovered that the rock star was wearing a gold necklace inside his shirt — a necklace which was rubbing against the material and causing the elusive noise.

Questions:

"Without getting too technical, how are commercials made?"

Nicholas Omana says: "Representatives from the advertising agency and/or from the client company itself bring me a spot. I get as much information as possible from the client so I'll know exactly what he or she is trying to say in the copy. (What the copy says and what the client thinks the copy says are often two different things.) We cast the spot. Sometimes clients already have certain artists in mind or 'on hold,' and we have to use them. Usually it works out, especially if the talent is the regular spokes for the product.

"We have a recording session. We begin with a run-through, which gives everyone a chance to hear the latest rewrites and to prepare for the actual takes. The engineer adjusts the mike and sets levels on the equalizer to roll off or boost certain frequencies.

"We do a take. Even if the first take is a buy, we do several more right away for backup protection. First-take buys are rare; clients usually want to hear the copy read several different ways so they'll have something to choose from.

"We do even more takes over a longer period of time, especially if rewriting is still going on or there are technical problems.

"Once the talent has laid down the voice tracks to everyone's satisfaction, the artist goes home and the major part of the technical work begins. In post (post-production), the engineer mixes down (combines) the various voice, music and sound-effects tracks into a final product."

"How much of the technical stuff do I really need to know?"

Not a lot. Just enough to do your job professionally. Most of it you'll get from this book and, if anything else sparks your curiosity, you can always ask an expert. Just don't ask them when they are working. Like you, technical people don't take kindly to folks who break their concentration.

Nicholas makes an interesting point: "If you know too much, it can actually be a handicap or a distraction. Particularly if you have done production work yourself. If you're hired as talent, do that and nothing more. When you go into the studio, let it all go. Relinquish responsibility and let everybody do their own jobs."

"How long do sessions last?"

Anywhere from five minutes to several hours. Producers aren't asking you to do more takes for their health. They have legitimate reasons — technical problems, ongoing rewrites, hard-to-satisfy clients, etc. But they are always aware that time is money and the clock is ticking.

Every hour spent in a recording session means at least two hours of post to complete the job. That's why the producers don't want to keep you around any longer than they have to. Once you go, they've still got a lot more expensive work to do.

"What happens if I'm in a session and there's just too much copy to read in the specified amount of time?"

First, make sure that the problem is with the copy and not with you. One of the exercises in this Chapter will have you working with a stop watch to develop exact timing.

Unless the problem is clearly in the script, it falls on you to bring that copy in on time. Nicholas explains what happens if your readings are too long or too short.

"If you are under, the client yells at the producer: 'You owe me more time — I paid for it!' If you're over, the producer yells at the client: 'You're getting free time and I'm paying for it!'"

"I could probably bring the copy in on time if I quit breathing."

Don't do that. The world would be minus one very special voice-over artist. Ask the engineer or producer for help, just as we asked John Westmoreland for help with this question.

"If your breathing actually interferes with your reading of the copy (either because the copy itself is too long or because you have been miked 'breathy'), it is sometimes better to slow down just a bit and give yourself a small pause before and after your breathing. Keep the copy itself rolling along at a fairly good clip.

"In post, the breaths themselves can be taken out and the timing corrected. We can cut you down into something inhuman (because you're not breathing), but you'll sound perfectly fine because people accept unrealistically short audio pauses that they'd never buy if you were on camera."

Exercises:

Practice working with background music and/or sound effects. If you have access to two tape recorders, put various background sounds and music on one, then play it while superimposing copy on the second machine. Although you will probably not often record over music or other sound, this exercise will familiarize you with the process.

Learn to work with a stop watch. Practice exact timing in delivering copy. A thirty-second spot should come in at exactly thirty seconds. Air time is expensive and must be precisely filled. Often music and sound effects are added to a spot after you have recorded it, and the timing is critical.

Work with a stop watch until you develop an internal stop watch. The true professional can shave a second off a spot on command, without even glancing at a clock.

"One thing my D.J. work gave me," says Nicholas Omana, "was an internal clock. I didn't have to learn timing when I started studying voice-overs. I already had a stop watch in my head."

Before we get into the next chapter, where you will be developing a number of characters, it's time to ask — particularly if you are a nonactor — whether you are feeling at all self-conscious about becoming another person. If so, this exercise will help you get past that feeling. While standing, read a short piece of copy, then put it aside. Observe your reactions to the reading. What are you doing? What are you feeling? In a stream-of-consciousness flow, tape your thoughts and observations in a very loud voice. Do this for a good three minutes. Here's what one student said:

"Well, I'm just standing here, shifting from one foot to the other. Maybe I should be crushing grapes. ... I feel funny without a piece of paper in my hands. I've got my hands at my sides. Now they're clasped in front of me. ... I'm not used to staring at four walls — especially four walls that are staring right back at me. ... I wonder what it would feel like to be on a stage — like the Shubert where I saw CATS. I'd probably drop dead in front of that many people. ... Now I'm running one hand through my hair. What am I looking for — lice? ... I think I'll take my jacket off. It's getting pretty warm in here. There — it's off. ... Wouldn't you know? The phone's ringing. Well, tough. The machine'll get it. ... There — the machine got it. ... I've got to come up with a new message

— nobody believes that I'm 'not here right now.' They know damn well I'm here; I'm just not picking up. Everybody knows I'm here because I'm only on Chapter Three. They know that if I were on Chapter Ten, I'd be out auditioning somewhere. Yeah, and if I were out auditioning somewhere, I'd be scared to death. ... Gee, it's quiet when the phone's not ringing. ... I'm picking up my jacket again. Why am I doing that? I just took it off. Must be nerves. Susan says everyone has nerves. I'll bet she doesn't. Nerves of steel. Professionals don't get nervous, do they? Maybe they do. Maybe they're human, after all."

When you've pretty well run down, immediately grab that piece of copy and read it aloud — in character. You will find that this exercise not only raises your energy level, it also gets rid of the inhibitions that stand between you and the text, thus making you one with the copy.

This exercise will also work for you on an audition or in any situation where you feel uncomfortable. Always talk your feelings out loud if at all possible, but at least get in touch with your fears and they will often shrink from the size of Mount Everest to that of a speed bump.

If you've stuck to hard-sell commercials up till now, pick a soft parent/child spot and get comfortable doing it. If you tend to do soft sells, practice taping more active commercials. When that phone call comes for an audition — for a job that means $$$$ — you can't tell them: "Diapers?! Are you kidding? All I know how to sell are big rigs and bulldozers!"

Don't place limits on your learning or you will only limit your range and your career. Other people try to limit you enough anyway — don't do it to yourself.

Chapter Four

Other Voices

By now, you are fairly well acquainted with a few of your characters. When asked to do a teacher, you become that particular teacher you learned to visualize in Chapter Two, etc. But what about all the other people still inside you? How do you reach them? How do you develop other voices?

As Pat Fraley says, "The number of voices you do is actually the number of characters you do." And the more voices you do, the more chances you will have of working. For Pat, the bottom line is developing and keeping different characters, and in his wonderfully analytical and organized fashion, he has designed an excellent system for doing both.

The following are some of the exercises Pat uses to discover other voices. You may find that only one works for you, or maybe you will be comfortable doing all five. But try them all. As you do this process, something interesting will begin to happen. Since by now you are proficient in doing the Basic Process, the new sounds you make will automatically trigger more than just new voices for you — new people will come out of your imagination to go with those new voices.

1. Impressions.

Run through a list of stars and record your impressions of how they speak. With the help of an objective friend who has a good ear, decide which voices are interesting to develop.

Susan adds: "Don't stop at the gender barrier. If you are a man, do female celebrities, and if you are a woman, by all means do male celebrities. Out of these reaches on your part will come the most interesting character voices. For example, a man imitating Julia Child will produce a unique character, while a woman imitating John Wayne will also come up with someone different and special. This takes you way beyond the realm of straight spokes and enriches your stable of characters."

2. Center work.

Turn on your tape recorder and just let it run while you do this physical exercise.

Center your attention on a particular part of your body and talk from there. How? Imagine there is a thorn in your nose. Focus only on that thorn and start talking. Talk about how it feels to have that thorn up your nose. It doesn't matter what you say; it's the feeling that counts. Later, in playback, you will probably hear a pinched, nasal, agitated voice.

Next, imagine there is a huge, soft sponge in your stomach. The sponge soaks up everything in sight and keeps getting bigger and bigger. Focus only on that sponge and start talking from the feeling of it. Have you discovered a rolling, heavy, slow kind of character?

Notice how the process of choosing and speaking from a center will automatically result in different characters as well as different placements for your voice. Go all out with this exercise. Work on placing that voice everywhere from the top of your head to the tips of your toes. See how many characters you can add to your repertory.

3. Inanimate objects.

Keep that tape recorder running as you look around the room and select particular objects. Become those objects. Start describing yourself as each one and how it feels to be that object.

Let's say you picked that old armchair right in front of you. Become the chair and start talking. You might say something like: *"I am a very old armchair. My upholstery is fading and I'm sagging all over because I'm old and so many people have sat down on me. I don't mind them sitting down, but I do mind when they put their feet up on me. Nobody would dare do that when I was new!"* Later, in playback, you might find you've discovered a crotchety, peevish, old character.

Try being a ceiling light bulb. When Molly Ann did this exercise, her light bulb said: *"I'm a bedroom ceiling light. Those people down there don't know it, but I'm watching them. I'm watching everything they do. Oh, wow! You wouldn't believe what they're doing now! They could get arrested for that! Hey, wait! Wait! Don't turn me off! I can't see anything if you close my eye!"* This gave Molly Ann a nosey voyeur type of character (as well as a reputation she's having trouble living down).

Susan's variation to this exercise is to imitate the sounds of inanimate objects and let voices emerge from those sounds. For example, make like a creaking door and then start to talk, keeping that same sound quality in your voice. You'll probably get an old crone or a witch.

4. Animals.

Become various animals, and talk about which animal you are and how it feels. Be a monkey, for example, and chatter away into your tape recorder. You probably will get a small, nervous, twitchy kind of character.

Next, be a gorgeous, long-haired cat and see if you don't come up with a serene, languid and dignified character. Susan suggests you try something similar to her inanimate object exercise. Make the sound of a certain animal and let a voice come right out of that sound. Susan did this with the "Baaaa" of a sheep and got a wonderful Katharine Hepburn-like character.

5. TV-logue.

Pat Fraley began his career in Australia where he taught Vocal Dynamics at an Australian university. Pat created the following exercise as a way of keeping his students' minds off their voices as they developed new characters.

Place your mike approximately halfway between you and your television set. Turn on the TV and the tape recorder, and imitate every sound and voice you hear on that channel. After ten or fifteen seconds on each, change channels, recording everything you hear. Don't stop for anything; just keep going until you run out of time, breath or sanity. Seriously, this is a very demanding exercise, and we recommend you spend only ten minutes or so at a time doing it.

Note: This is a different exercise from the one in Chapter Two, in which you turned off the TV sound completely and went for the mood or quality of the picture.

Not only can you come up with even more characters this way, but you can also hear how closely you imitate many different sounds and voices. Another benefit is that you can hear your own mix as your voice is recorded with background music and sound effects.

Now that you are finding all sorts of new people, it is most important that you have a way of remembering them. You must be able to become each one at a moment's notice and hit the mark every time.

Pat Fraley's solution is to fill out a Character Voice Catalog Sheet for each of his characters. The sheets are kept on file and altered or updated as needed. Pat's character sheets contain the following information:

Character's Name.

Always name your characters. If you do a terrific Bob Newhart impression, you would probably want to name that character Bob Newhart. If the character is one whom you have created from a less identifiable source, invent a name that you will immediately associate with that character. To name the dignified, serene voice of that gorgeous, long-haired cat you worked with earlier, you might want to call her, *Cat*herine the Great, or him, S*cat*man The Magnificent — whatever, as long as it identifies that character to you.

Source of the Character.

How did you find the character? Knowing your source can help you recall the character as you recall the process by which you found him or her.

Key phrase.

This is a wonderful, quick way to get back into character. Write a phrase which is very typical of each character. The Dignified Cat might say: "I can't be bothered right now — I'm busy being beautiful." With practice, you can get to the point where you won't need to put on the character item by item as we did in Chapter Two; simply say the key phrase and you will be that character.

Comments.

Add any and all information that helps you to identify the character. If your character comes from the image of an old armchair in your grandparents' home, make a note of that. If your character has certain mannerisms, list them. One woman we know is a good amateur artist. She makes a little sketch of each of her characters as a visual aid to identifying them.

Wherever your new characters come from — once they do show up, don't let them go! Make friends with each and every one. Name them, categorize them, and know everything there is to know about them. Practice being them until you can quickly and easily get into each character.

Vocal Elements.

Pat further categorizes his characters by determining the following six vocal elements for each one.

1. Pitch.

This has to do with the musical note of the voice. Is the voice high or low? It can also be labeled tenor, soprano, bass, or alto.

2. Pitch Characteristic.

Tone refers to the quality of the pitch. It can be rough, breathy, clear, metallic, harsh, gravelly, etc.

3. Tempo.

Does the character speak slowly or quickly? A nervous little monkey would speak with a much faster tempo than a big, lumbering polar bear.

4. Rhythm.

Is the speech syncopated, lilting, pedantic, etc.? This is not the same as tempo; the character can speak with a slow tempo, yet maintain either a lilting or a syncopated rhythm.

5. Placement.

Where does the voice seem to be coming from? Speak as the character and imagine where that voice is centered. Be very specific. Does the voice seem to come from the back of the throat, the tip of the nose, or is it closer to the bridge of the nose?

6. Mouth Work.

What are you doing with your mouth to make the character sound different than your normal voice? Does the character have an accent? If so, is the dialect heavy or light?

Dialects are usually the last refinement you add to a voice. Pat recommends that you always start with your own voice when you practice a dialect. Once you have the dialect, then you can layer it onto other voices you are experimenting with.

Let's talk about accents for a moment. How do you get an accent? Voice-over artist and director Philip L. Clarke, a recognized expert in accents and dialects, says that perhaps the worst place to go looking for accents is old movies. Although you can find a few actors who were actually from other countries and who had genuine foreign accents, most actors vocalized what they thought a particular accent should sound like.

Philip emphasizes that accents "must be authentic. The more authentic they are, the more believable you are. But don't make the accent too thick or you'll lose your audience. The idea is to 'get' the full accent, then 'bring it down' to the point where you can be understood." And where do you get the accent? If you are not able to go to the actual locale, then seek out people who are from the region or country whose accent you wish to learn. Airports, ethnic restaurants and cultural centers are excellent places to find these people. Ask them questions; get them talking; then listen to them speak. Watch their mouths to see where sounds are placed. Tape them if you can for later reference. Philip feels most dialect records and tapes on the market are a less satisfactory way of learning accents because they can't give you the visuals of an accent — the sound placements and especially the mannerisms that accompany the actual language.

Mannerisms? Most definitely! As Philip says: "It is not enough just to 'do' an accent. You also must create a body for that accent to live in." For credibility's sake, never let an accent come out of your mouth without having one of your characters do the talking.

Keep mimicking the speakers you are studying until you know exactly how they would say something without first having to hear them say it. And practice! One of Philip's favorite exercises is to take a magazine (*Time*, for example) that carries articles about many different countries, and to read each article aloud, using that country's particular accent.

Animation work generally calls for caricatures of accents as opposed to the more realistic accents used in commercials. But, as Philip points out: "In either case you must be completely believable in terms of authenticity of accent and character."

It is not unusual for directors to ask to hear another voice. Advertising people often ask for a spokesperson. All they really want is to hear one or more of your characters speak — as living, breathing, real people. This means that you must be so familiar with your characters and their attitudes that you can comfortably ad lib for a minute or so as each one. Just remember to keep it natural — believe who you are, and they will believe it, too.

Examples of Demo Tape boxes.

Examples of Demo Tape box labels.

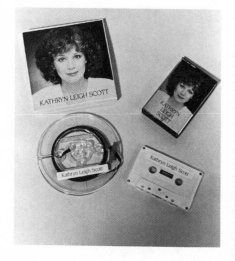

Director Andrea Romano briefs voice-over artists in the lounge of
Voicetrax West before recording the Word of Mouth audio tape.

On the air! Director Romano and engineer/actor Nicholas
Omana at the console recording voice-over artists Susan Blu,
Michael Sheehan and Molly Ann Mullin in the booth.

A fluffed line brings a chuckle from Director Andrea Ramano.

Engineer Nicholas Omana concentrates on levels and mixes.

Director and engineer at the Tascam 50 eight-track console.
A Teac 80 eight-track recorder is on a shelf above
two Tascam 32 two-track decks.

Beau Weaver

Susan Blu

Michael Sheehan

Jennifer Darling

Samantha Paris

Molly Ann Mullin

Thom Pinto

Pat Musick

Mary McDonald Lewis

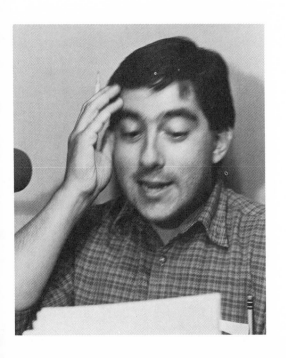

Nicholas Omana

A very crowded recording booth. L-R: Pat Musick, Mary McDonald Lewis, Jennifer Darling, Beau Weaver, Samantha Paris, Thom Pinto and Nicholas Omana.

Chapter Five

Animation

THE MANY VOICES IN YOU

Although there are many similarities in the techniques used to attain excellence in both commercial and animation work, the latter really warrants a study all its own. Susan, a veteran animation performer who now casts and directs animated series, has put together a video based on her training seminars. This chapter will introduce you to the world of animation and give you a taste of what's involved in creating cartoon voices.

If commercial voice-overs required you to shed a few inhibitions and do a moderate stretch to become a Reassuring Attorney or a Concerned Shopper, now you must really reach to become a Shy Unicorn or a Wicked Monster. Molly Ann admits: "We know all about jitters; believe me, we've had them! But if you do manage to shed all remaining inhibitions and take the plunge into this fantastically creative and thrilling world, you won't regret it and you won't ever look back."

The most important thing to remember in discovering all those people who live inside you, is to give yourself permission TO PLAY. When Susan was in school, she used to hide behind her characters. They spoke so she didn't have to, and she made many a trip to the principal's office for trying to impersonate someone in her class. What was then forbidden and punished is now a rewarding profession and a lucrative way of life.

"To find cartoon voices," Susan says, "is to leave your Adult outside the door and find that uninhibited Child inside you. And you won't get kicked out of class for doing it either! Too bad we didn't realize we weren't 'bad' back then — our inhibitions might not be as strong as they are now."

This is probably not the first time you have created a character. You did it with consummate ease and grace when you were a child. When you spoke the words of the Beautiful Princess or the Super Hero, you absolutely believed you were those characters and so you became them. You worked instinctively, from the inside out, starting with your belief in the existence of the character and then adding a voice, body language, attitudes and sometimes even a costume and props to go with it. The result? A dynamic, fully-developed character was born.

As an adult, you may also have created characters, particularly if you ever read to a child. Can you honestly say you didn't play all the parts in the story? You couldn't help but make the Dragon sound big and threatening, or maybe cute and klutzy and kind. Your Baby Rabbit was little and scared, or laughing and excited — all for the benefit of those wide, wondering eyes and those eager ears that were hanging on your every word. Perhaps you worked in children's theater and brought characters to life by interpreting them with all the belief and drama that were in the colors of the costume you wore. Maybe you just swapped secrets with a special friend at camp many years ago, or told scary ghost stories at slumber parties after football games.

In whatever tales you told or acted out over the years, the voices you used animated the stories. You shared characters that were a part of you and that fond memory, recent or past, has inspired you now to do cartoons. The techniques we'll discuss will help you re-learn what you knew how to do instinctively as a child.

Where to begin? First, pick a safe and quiet work place where you won't be interrupted and then ... giggle. Good. Now giggle some more. Let that giggle grow bigger and bigger until it bursts out of you in a hearty belly laugh. Feels great, doesn't it?

Now fill your mind with ghouls and goblins, and listen to the ghost laugh that comes out of you. Go directly into the vocal sound of this laugh, saying: "Halloween is coming and I'm going to scare everybody who crosses my path!" There — you just animated your voice! You created a character, a Something-That-Goes-Bump-in-the-Night, from a simple laugh.

There are all sorts of ways to come up with cartoon voices and we will cover many of them in this introductory chapter. Notice you did not change your voice by simply "changing your voice." Instead, you changed your voice by changing what was going on inside you. The amateur's mistake is to find a voice for the character rather than finding the character itself. As with commercial voice-overs, you must become the character. The voice can't help but follow.

Suppose you want to play a little elf. Visualize the elf you want to be. Let's say it is a little boy elf. You don't want him to sound old, but don't just think of him as "young." See him at a particular age. Five? Nine? Twelve? You have the freedom and the fun of choosing. Now suppose you know this elf boy has a rough and tumble attitude, but you want him to be even more aggressive. Just picture him being the toughest elf in the forest — the one with all the wood chips on his shoulder — and he'll automatically sound like a real heavy. Want him to sound nasal? Give him a head cold and feel the congestion. Want him to sound a little silly? Give him an overbite.

Visualization is the key to creating characters. Learn everything you can about the personality and the physicality of the person you are becoming. Delve into the heart and soul of the character and you will organically create its voice. Amateurs speak from the neck up. Excellent voice-over actors speak from the hearts and souls of the characters they know so intimately.

While visualization is essential for achieving excellence in voice-over animation, it may be enhanced by using certain other techniques, such as placement.   When we speak in a normal voice, we are in the mid-range of our vocal instrument. When we become nervous or upset, our voice has a tendency to rise in pitch. On a blissfully stress-free day or after a thoroughly relaxing massage, the voice is usually lower and deeper. We can manipulate different placements ourselves to ensure the characters we create continue speaking in their wonderful voices.

There are ten standard vocal placements. Practice each one carefully and see how comfortable you can become with each one before moving on to the next. As with the other exercises in this book, take your time and don't overdo it or you'll wind up with a sore throat. Your vocal chords are muscles; treat them like you would any other muscle in your body. Just as you wouldn't run a 10K race cold without building up your leg muscles, don't force your vocal chords beyond their limits. Let them build slowly and surely, as you build a solid foundation for your talent.

1. The head voice.

Men, try impersonating a female. Ladies, think of doing Julia Childs. Let that voice fill your head and rattle around in there until it knows it's found a home.

2. The eyes.

Here are Susan's tips for this placement: "I always think of Hayley Mills in the movie POLLYANNA. She had a very youthful sound that was airy, up and innocent. Also, try thinking of sunshine coming through your eyes. It feels quite bright and British."

3. Nasal.

Speak very frontally right through your nose. Pinch your nostrils with your fingers and say "hello," then let go and try to duplicate that nasal sound. You will probably sound like you have a bad cold — and this is good.

4. Adenoidal.

This is the sound of a bad cold having a bad day. You are the most plugged up you will ever be. Located far back in the nasal cavity, this voice sounds as if your entire head is filled with tissue paper.

5. Near the ears.

Remember the Munchkins in THE WIZARD OF OZ? Imitate them now by singing: "Oh, we're off to see the Wizard, the wonderful Wizard of Oz." Can you feel your ears vibrate? That delightful bubbly sound coming out of you is very cartoony, but extremely lovable.

6. Lower mouth.

Recapture that plugged-up adenoidal feeling, but bring the voice down into the mouth for a mushy sound. Make sure your cheeks are loose and your jaw is flexible. This particular placement has been used for all sorts of cute characters. The "Muttley" Daws Butler created for Hanna-Barbera immediately comes to mind.

7. The throat.

Drop your voice into your throat and growl. Very good. Now growl the growl of an Evil Ruler on the brink of losing his kingdom and say: "No one will ever take my kingdom from me — no one!" And *voilà* — you have created a terrific Villain.

8. Back of the throat.

Move your voice towards the back of your throat and say the word "hello." It should sound like Pee Wee Herman or Kermit the Frog, and is a great voice for nerds, little animals and even certain thugs.

9. Chest.

Place your voice squarely in your chest and try the word "hello." Did that solid, upright greeting surprise you? It's a natural for honest and sincere heroes and heroines.

10. The diaphragm.

This placement will give you your deepest and strongest voice. It is the sound of power and authority, and it speaks convincingly as either Good or Evil.

Character voices other than the ones we've described will come to you as you practice these exercises, but remember: The voice is only a small part of the total character. A cute or interesting voice does not make a great cartoon character. You must develop the complete character by visualizing its totality because your job is to make it jump off the page and bring it to life.

Susan, who has directed a number of cartoon shows, has this to say: "Many times when I've been casting, the actor will ask me what I'm looking for. Much of the time we don't know. We may have a good understanding of the character's personality, but often we don't have a specific sound in mind. If you are the one who brings that character to life, we will know it when we hear it."

And speaking of hearing it, how many things don't we hear in the course of an ordinary day? We don't really listen to the blender as it whips up our favorite protein drink. We cringe and block out the motorcycle that roars down our streets. We hurry to slap the ringing alarm clock into silence. We live in a vacuum of sound. But the sounds of the inanimate objects around us are great for helping us find cartoon characters.

Consider the blender. Imitate its whirring, then layer-in words to that sound. Perhaps you came up with the voice of a big, buzzing insect. Maybe you found a different character. As long the character you discovered is interesting and believable, it's worth keeping. Listen to the world around you. Imitate its many sounds and let your imagination run wild and free in discovering more characters.

Animal sounds can also help you come up with many unique and vivid characters to add to your growing *repertoire*. (Visualization, of course, will flesh them out.) Take the sound of a lamb. That "baaaaa" is a great way to produce the voice of an old man or old lady. Try it now. It might also give you a nervous, insecure character. Work with a variety of animal sounds to explore characters that could speak with those voices.

Another way to find characters is through celebrity impersonations. Here's Susan's success story using this technique: "There was a show that Marvel was doing called MOONDREAMERS. After they had seen every guy in town, they got the idea to audition some women. I was one of those women. The character they described to me was very much like a soldier. He wore a little helmet and he spoke with great authority. I felt he might be similar to George C. Scott's portrayal in PATTON, but I knew if I told the casting director I wanted to do George C. Scott, I would have been laughed out of the studio. So I just did it. I gave them my version of Scott's Patton, with a heart, a soul and a personality. I had such a clear image of who the character was, I created a complete cartoon entity. And I got the job."

Now you've been cast in an animated show. Congratulations! Know that when you go in to play the part for which you've been cast, you may also be asked to do another role. Animation is a multi-voice business. You may wind up doing as many as three different voices. You'll receive one fee for the first two and an additional ten percent for the third voice. Everybody generally makes the same rate whether they do five lines or fifty.

You may work only one and one-half hours, but you are required to be available for four hours under SAG rules. You will make about a thousand dollars for each episode in which you have performed one or more voices.

This is also a very fast business. While it takes one week to do a 22-minute on-camera sitcom, you will tape a 22-minute animation show in four hours or less. As Molly Ann puts it: "When time is so important, you can't be average and you can't be erratic; you must be consistently excellent to make it in voice-overs, commercial or animation."

The following is a list of characters we recommend you develop, and we recommend you develop two voices for each character. Why? After you have been booked to do a guest spot and you are in the studio with other actors preparing to record, you may hear another performer speak in a voice similar to the one you were planning on using. You must be able to come up with another voice ON THE SPOT. If you know your characters inside and out, this won't be a problem.

Hero/Heroine	Butler
Nanny	Sea Captain
Villain/Villainess	Elf
Nurse	Gun Moll
Little Furry Animal	Gremlin
Pirate	Irish Policeman

Robot	Bookworm
Witch	Grandmother
High Society Woman	Bug
Unicorn	Grandfather
School Principal	Teenager
Baby	

Remember the laugh exercise we did at the beginning of this chapter? Do it now for all these characters. Remember to picture each character you're working on. Tape the exercise and then listen to hear whether each character has a laugh all its own. Once the characters' laughs are distinct and can be summoned up quickly and easily, start speaking in their different voices.

Borrow children's books from the library and read them aloud. Tape your efforts and listen to them. Do you believe those characters really exist? Leave messages on your answering machine in different voices. While driving in your car, make up situations for your characters and let them speak the appropriate dialogue. Susan watches old movies on TV and then re-creates the characters' voices. "I try to climb inside each interesting character," she says. "Actually I get to know them, feel what they're feeling, and the voices just come."

Both animation and commercial voice-overs require you to bring a character to life. But when you walk into that lonely, probably cold and intimidating booth, your nerves and your surroundings may conspire to do you in. Here's where your imagination and visualization skills can help you succeed.

First of all, pretend that you are not in the booth. Let the setting of the story be your setting. If the tale is one of knights and dragons, let the booth be the castle you're defending from the raging beast. Or let it be the clearing in the forest where you'll fry that nasty old knight with one blast of your flaming breath. If the story is about fairies granting wishes, let the booth be your magic dreamland of marvelous wishes come true.

See the colors of the scenery you've chosen and add as many wonderful details as you can to set the stage for the arrival of your characters. Give them a special place in which to be, then bring them to life by creating their hearts and souls. Don't just "do" voices. Lots of people can do voices; only the best can come up with three-dimensional characters.

For an example of some of the finest animated voice work, watch old Warner Bros.' LOONEY TOONS and listen to the brilliant talent of the late

Mel Blanc doing his famous Bugs Bunny, Porky the Pig, Daffy Duck, Sylvester, and various other characters. Notice that the voice placements for his characters are quite similar, but the distinct personalities he gave each one created unique, unmistakeable individuals that we immediately recognize.

Bugs Bunny is very cocky and self-assured. We believe that he believes he can get himself out of every tough situation. Porky is shy, adorable and insecure. Mel even gave him a stutter to finesse the character. Sylvester has a frontal lisp and Daffy has a lateral one — further refinements on already well-established characters. Mel's creations came out of his personality and heart, so they in turn had unique and believable identities. The industry and the world miss this great man, but his very real and vivid characters live on and on.

Is there a place in the world of animation voice-overs for you? There most certainly is — if you are willing to work hard to master the techniques we've described in this chapter and in this book. Perseverance will get you in the door; your talent and your training will allow you to stay there. And you can't just be good, you must be excellent.

Some additional thoughts from Susan: "When I directed JAMES BOND, JUNIOR, I must have seen over two hundred actors for six different roles. The competition is fierce, but we are always looking for fresh, new talent. I used several actors that season who were brand new to this art form, but they all had several things in common. Each had a *repertoire* of characters ranging from heroes to villains to butlers to maids. Many different characters in all shapes and sizes were just straining to come out of the actors and find a place on a show. The actors had been finding and developing all these people who lived inside them for such a long time, and now they were ready to introduce them to the world of animation. There is nothing more exciting than discovering new talent brimming over with with full-blown and complete characters."

Voices came easy to us as children. We knew we were the Cowboy, so we could say with absolute conviction: "This town just ain't big enough for the two of us." We believed all those characters we portrayed. We were those characters, so their voices were true. The years passed and, sadly, "growing up" silenced our many voices. Fortunately, animation voice-overs allow us to recapture that spirit — that uninhibited, creative spark which illuminated our childhood worlds — and people this larger, often lonely adult world with an abundance of gifts from our hearts and souls.

The following are excerpts from the animation demo scripts of Jan Rabson, Kevin Shon and Mona Marshall. These wonderfully talented voice-over artists have generously agreed to let us share this material with you.

ADVENTURES IN SPACE

by Mona Marshall

(1940s PIANO)

ANNOUNCER   Good evening, Ladies and Gentle-
men and welcome to Mellow
Drama's Live Radio Theatre
brought to you tonight from the
terribly chic, too, too sleek
and cheeky, posh and peaky,
Sportmen's Lodge Lounge, where
the high, low and in between
mingle amidst the tingle of almost crystal, at least it's
glass not plastic, and the conversation ranges from the auda-
ciously austere to the morbidly
mundane. Please note: Unlike
the name suggests, there are no
animal heads adorning the
walls, perhaps the tables from
time to time on a particularly
raucous evening...but not the
walls. Instead we have our own
sweet sight of serenity: Sam,
the supple and sagacious swan.
(POINT TO SAM). But enough
about ambiance and atmosphere
and on with our show.

ANNOUNCER   Tonight, we bring you a story
                     of subtle strength, (STING) of
                     super-human struggle, (STING)
                     of science fiction supremacy.
                     (STING) A saga so superior in
                     its scope, so sublime in its
                     summation that it stuns the
                     senses. Tonight, Ladies and Gen-
                     tlemen, we bring you (BIG ROLL)
                     Sheldon and Sheila Soloman's
                     sensational best selling short
                     story, now a radio serial.

ADVENTURES IN
SPACE   (ORGAN
THEME)
                     But, first a word from our
                     sponsor. ("NBC CHIME")

(SWEET FLOW-
ING MUSIC)

COMMERCIAL   Hello. Is your love life less
                     than lustful? Is your lover's
                     libido lacking or lost? Is your
                     heart hungering for a handsome
                     hunk that isn't hamburger?
                     ...If that's the problem, your
                     solution is to give him every-
                     thing you are...NOTHING. (STOP
                     MUSIC) Yes. Wear NOTHING and
                     he'll be eating out of your ...
                     hand. (NOTHING STING)

ANNOUNCER   And now... ADVENTURES IN ...
                     SPACE...(ORGAN THEME)

(HEROIC MUSIC)

NARRATOR   It is the year 2090 A.D. A
             group of intergalactic young-
             sters and their teachers are
             traveling in their vehicular
             space module, heading toward
             the moon on a routine lunar ex-
             pedition, when suddenly and in-
             explicably their flight pattern
             is altered and they are forced
             to land on a hitherto unknown
             planet. (ROCKET CRASH)

(EERIE SPACE
MUSIC)

TOMMY   Wow, look at this place. Hey,
             this might even be more excit-
             ing than an old moon expedition.

KENJI   Ah, Tommy-san, is this cool or
             what? We don't even need "Wet"
             suits.

MOGO   Yo, homeboy Kenji, that's
             weight suit!

KENJI   That's what I said, "Weight
             suit."

MOGO   In that case you said it right.
             This here's badder than a lunar
             flight.

ALEXANDER   I don't know if that is a valid
             evaluation of our situation,

MoGo. According to my calcula-
tions we are approximately
1,729 kilometers past the fif-
teenth triad parallel which I
deduce to mean that...

BENJY   Whoa ... We could be in big,
               big trouble. I don't know, you
               guys. It looks kinda scary to
               me. Those are weird looking
               trees. The branches look like
               giant bony fingers that could
               reach out and grab us.

MEG   Don't worry, Benjy. Do remem-
               ber, we're all junior explor-
               ers. We'll simply look at this
               as another deliriously deli-
               cious deviation from the dol-
               drums.

MICHAEL   That's right, Meg, the only
               thing we have to worry about
               is...Where in the Universe are
               we? (STING)

SUZANNA   Oh, Michael, you have to be
               just about the finest specimen
               of young manhood I've ever
               seen. Cross my heart and hope
               to have hushpuppies...Oooo, you
               are magnificent! I do hope
               there's a quiet place for us to
               be alone.

VAL   Oooo, Yeah, Mikey Babes, you
               are definitly a TRD, as in To-
               tally Rad Dude. Oooo, this

place is really weird. I wonder
if they have a shopping mall
and if they do, if they'll take
credit cards.

SURFLEY   Whoa, Val, good point! I wonder
if they've some gnarly waves
here, too. Bitchin'! (MUSIC OUT)

MAJOR GERMACK   Alright you little Rocket Rats,
quickly gather 'round the space
vehicle ... the captain has
something she wants to tell you.

CAPTAIN   Junior Explorers, due to a technical snafu beyond our control,
we've had to make an unsched-
uled landing on what looks to
be in my estimation some ...
tough turf. So while we adults
explore the area, you children
are to stay here with the space-
craft.

CHILDREN   Aw, aw, aw, aw, aw, aw, Bummer.

LT. CHEKOV   Calm yourselves, my little Com-
rades, there is much work to do
here. We will leave Kiko the
Computer and Miko the Mutant
Maltese to help you.

KIKO   Thank you, Lt. Checkov, your
verbal expression of confidence
is appreciated and has been
filed under compliment.

MIKO   (Gurgle-growl) Compliment nice,
                but Miko want a cookie.

MARGARET   Here, Miko, we can share.

MIKO   (Gobble) All gone. Miko no like
                to share. Miko need walk.

MARGARET   Okay, as soon as the adults
                leave I'll take you for a walk
                over by that dark, scary cave
                ... maybe we can find some Mon-
                sters! (Giggle)

MIKO   No way, what are you? Nuts!

(NEW EERIE
MUSIC)

NARRATOR   And, as we leave our seemingly
                secure and serene scene of
                space survivors, we see that
                some unsavory sub-human species
                have been spying on our unsus-
                pecting subjects. (STING)

EVIL 1   Oh, look, looky, looky there ...

EVIL 2   Oh, yes, Mistress, your prestig-
                ious plot is working precisely
                as you planned.

EVIL 3   Oh, yes, oh, yes, oh, yes ...
                the adults are leaving the chil-
                dren unguarded ... Goody,
                goody, goody!

MISTRESS   Ooooohhhm shut up, you Slobber-
                  ing Simpletons, those brats are
                  not unguarded, they have their
                  radically advanced, K12 KO Z
                  Computer and their stupidly af-
                  fectionate pet Mutant Maltese
                  to protect them! Oh, Dratted
                  Sunshine and Lightness, how I
                  hate those sickeningly loveable
                  beasts with their insatiable ap-
                  petites for sweets!

EVIL PET   Mistress is right, The computer
                  can sense us and warn them of
                  our presence and their beast
                  could pierce through our
                  hearts, and kill us with kind-
                  ness ... and calories. (STING)

ALL EVIL   Ah, ah, ah, ah, ah...

MISTRESS   Ahhhh, we must get them before
                  they discover us and uncover
                  ... THE SECRET!

NARRATOR   And what, you may ask sitting
                  there in your comfortable
                  chair, is the dark and nefari-
                  ous secret these mysterious min-
                  ions of evil embrace so closely
                  to their breasts? And will they
                  adopt any arduous implements of
                  terrifying torture to subdue
                  the spirit, not to mention the
                  bodies, of our spunky space sur-
                  vivors?

ANNOUNCER	For the answer to these questions, and many more, tune in again next week for: ADVENTURES IN SPACE ... (SPACE THEME) Until then, good night and good musing.

PART TWO

ANNOUNCER	Good evening, Ladies and Gentlemen, and welcome to part 2 of Adventures in Space.
NARRATOR	When last we left our spunky space survivors, they were about to be detrimentally detered by those malevolent minions of maliciousness. But fear not, no, indeed, you see, more sociable, solicitous species have been spying on the spies.
GOOD 1	Oh my, it looks like those poor children may need our help.
GOOD 2	Oh my dear, you're absolutely right.
GOOD 3	Yes, we're talking major evil here. The kind of dire diehard decadence and deceit we are dedicated to destroy and defeat with due diligence ... in other words ... no dallying ... those darlings are in desperate despair ... They could get dumped on!

GOOD 4   Yeah, let's savage the suckers!

NARRATOR   So will those gritty, gallant
                Good Gals indeed savage the
                suckers? Or will the sweet un-
                suspecting space survivors es-
                cape the unsavory sub-human
                species that would subject them
                to a fate worse than swallowing
                slimy, salty salamanders?

ANNOUNCER   Tune in again next week at the
                same time to find out the an-
                swer to that question and many
                more as we bring you the next
                episode of ... ADVENTURES IN
                SPACE ...

                Good night and good musing.

AUDITION SCRIPT
by Kevin Shon

STEVE (Hand-   Hi, Wendy! Gosh, uh, you look
some Jock, 17   really terrific tonight! Uh,
years old)   what I mean is...You always
                look terrific! Hey, we better
                get going. We're gonna miss the
                kickoff!

PROFESSOR   Oooh, I've forgotten the spell
STUBBINS   again...Uh, let's see...Three
(Kindly wiz-   F's...Uh...Fee...Fi...Fo...Oh,
ard, 66 years   no, that's not it...Uh...Full
old)   fathom five..My father...No,
                no, no!

Uh...Eh...Fee..Uh...Fi...Uh...Fo.
..Ooooh Fiddlesticks!

FIM-WHIMSY   (Giggle) Silly! Why, this isn't
(Mischievous   just any old forest...This is a
elf)   magic forest! Anything can hap-
                      pen here!

MR. SPINGE   Why, hello, my dear...What's a
(Seductive   nice...plump...tasty-looking
villain)   little thing like you doing in
                      the middle of the deep, dark
                      forest? Aren't you afraid to be
                      out here all by yourself?

BUDDY (Dopey   Oh, boy...Somebody ate the blue-
little bear)   berry bundt cake I baked for
                      Billy Beasley's birthday. Oh,
                      now what am I going to do?

MARVIN   (Fran- Can I come with you, Professor?
tic nerd)   Huh, can I, huh, huh? I won't
                      get in the way. I won't touch
                      anything this time, I promise.
                      Oh, please, say yes, say yes,
                      say yes, say yes, PLEASE say
                      yes!

ERNIE (Rowdy,   Howdy, mah name is Ernie and
rough and   I'm a cowboy hairdresser! Yep,
tough cowpoke)   that's right. Cowboys like to
                      look good, too! 'Course, they
                      don't like it to get around, so
                      keep it under your hat!

MAYOR BOFF   My fellow limptoads! Today is a
(Pompous blow-   day that will live forever in
hard)   limptoad history! Uh...yes.

That is, eh...hysterically, I
mean, HISTORICALLY speaking.
I'm talking about...eh...what
am I talking about?

LITTLE BOO (Adorable 8 year old) — Oh, gee, I don't think we should go in there. It looks awfully dark and spooky. And what's that awful smell? Oh! I think I hear my mom calling me. I have to go home now! Bye!

BELDAR (Hero-a bit too full of himself) — Don't despair, Princess! I will lead you through the labyrinth and return you safely to Gaffonia. Put your arms around my neck and hold on tightly.
(Choking)
Not...quite...that...tightly...

NICK (Tough Bronx Italian, 35 years old) — Hey, how you doin'? Yer listenin' ta Nick, on W.A.R.T., Yer arts and classics station. Comin' up next...Da first movement of Cosi Fan Tutti. So...get yer fan tutti cozy, and we'll be right back.

WINKY (Snooty scientist) — Obviously you don't have the slightest idea what I'm talking about. (Sigh) Very welllll...Pay attention and I'll see if I can't explain this in a way that even YOU can understand.

BRATLEY (Snotty little brat) — Oh wait, wait, don't tell me, I know. The numerator is on the

top and the denominator is on
the bottom, huh? Whaddya ya
mean that's not right? OK,
fine, the denominator is on the
top and the numerator is on the
bottom. Ahhh, who cares anyway?!

O'HAVER   Hah, hah, hah, hah, hah, hah!
(Big, dumb   Dat'll teach ya' to get outta
jerk of a dog)   da way, punk! Ha, ha, ha, ha,
                 ha! Awwwww...Did he hurt his
                 widdle paw? What a dweeb! What
                 a doofus! What a weenie dawg!
                 Ha, ha, ha, ha!

GRAMPS   Would you just look at this
(Grumpy old   mess! Those little blue bozos
man)   have really done it this time!
                 That does it! I'm gonna get my
                 fly swatter and go pay those
                 little pipsqueaks a visit!

AUNTIE ETHEL   (Sings) "I'm in the mood for
Wacky witch,   looove...Simply because you're
alwayslookin'   near me...and every time you're
for love)   near me, I'm in the mood for
                 love." Come on honey, let's
                 smooch! Kiss me, you fool, or
                 I'll turn you into a slug!

HANNA-BARBERA AUDITION
by Jan Rabson

ROD SERLING   Witness if you will, a world of animation. A new dimension of sight and sound. You are about to enter a different realm where reality and fantasy take on new aspects. There's a sign-post up ahead - Jan Rabson doing a 3- to-5-minute voice-over audition at Hanna-Barbera zone.

NARRATOR   Once upon a time...

NERD   Hey, this sounds like a fairy tale.

NARRATOR   Not quite...in a land far away known as Larynxland, there lived a king named...

NERD   Tonsilectomy (Laugh)

NARRATOR   Who, pray tell, are you?

NERD   Oh, hi, I'm Nerd Guard Jr. and I go to Northridge College to study accounting so I can be like my father, well, not really, because I want to own my own firm, see, and he works for, like, a small little company, although he has his own secretary which is pretty cool...

NARRATOR   Are you quite through?

NERD   I think so.

NARRATOR   Every year there was a...

TEENAGER   It's my turn. Every year there
                was an Ugliest Man in the King-
                dom contest. The winner got
                10,000 Dulmas—that's about 160
                dollars. All the ugly men lined
                up and the king judged the win-
                ner.

OLD BRIT   Why, there they are, ugly
                brutes. Reminds me of the time
                I was in New Guinea—or was it
                Rhodesia? The natives were
                rather restless—or were they on
                the warpath? No matter, there
                was tension in the air—or was
                it something else—maybe it was
                a small fever going about.

GOOD OL' BOY   Wow, you've been just about ev-
                erywhere and done everything.
                This is my first time watching
                one of these ugly contests.
                I'll bet you've seen a bunch,
                huh?

TERRY THOMAS   If I recall correctly, last
                year's contest was quite excit-
                ing. The gentlemen, and I use
                the term ever so loosely, was
                so ugly when he took off his
                hat that they arrested him for

carrying a concealed weapon.

EMCEE   And without any further ado, I
             present to you the man who gave
             you taxation without representa-
             tion, a mere figurehead, a bum-
             bling, inefficient monarch, an
             anachronism and a blight on the
             human race—your king.

THE KING   Oh, thank you, thank you. A
             very nice speech indeed. Ohhhh,
             my. Before we begin the con-
             test, are there any questions?

THE PRINCE   Yes. Your highness, could you
             tell me why every year we de-
             base and humiliate our fellow
             man in such an infantile and de-
             meaning manner?

THE KING   Who was that young snit?

EMCEE   Your son...the Prince, sire.

THE KING   Oh, I thought he looked famil-
             iar.

EAST INDIAN If I may be philosophic on the
             question put forth by this
             young and quite inquisitive
             lad, the contest is merely
             a...Hey, what are you doing?
             Put me down...leave me alone.

JEWISH   Look, the ugly persons are lin-
             ing up, and so painful to look
             at. Speaking of pain, this fin-

ger hurts me, but this finger
doesn't hurt me half as much as
this finger hurts me...

EMCEE   Take your places, please.

BIG DEEP VOICE I'm really not that ugly. I'm
only doing this contest til my
big break comes in show business...actually, I'm a dancer.

FRENCH   The fact is I am not ugly at
all. I am extremely handsome. I
know this, and this is what
makes me ugly. I am so con-
ceited and egotistical that people can't stand to be around me.

MEEK   I'm probably the ugliest person
here. I need that prize money.
It's been a dream of mine for
years to open up a shoe store
for hard-to-fit sizes.

BRONX   Hey, hold your horses...

BIG DEEP VOICE Was he referring to me?

BRONX   Look what I found. If this
ain't the ugliest guy I ever
saw I don't know what is. I had
to put a sack over his head he
was so beastly.

GRAVEL VOICE   You lousy, stupid, moronic
idiot. I'll see you're hung for
this! You'll never know another
minute of peace! I'll make your

life hell if it's the last
thing I do!

BRONX   He even talks ugly. It's per-
               fect.

BROOKLYN   I don't want to bust your bub-
               ble or nothing, but I got to
               tell you that the guy you got
               there ain't no ugly man, but an
               ugly woman...uh, I
               mean...that's the Queen!

THE PRINCE   Hey, that's my mom!

BRONX   You're kidding. Oh, I'm really
               sorry, your highness...I, uh, I
               didn't recognize you with the
               beard.

NARRATOR   And so our story ends. The King
               declared that the Queen was in-
               deed the winner of the contest.
               The man who found her was
               awarded 10,000 Dulmas. The
               Queen swore she would never
               speak to the King again, and
               the King...lived happily ever
               after.

Chapter Six

Tags and Doubles

Tags are a few words or short phrases that either end a piece of copy or stand alone to identify and describe a product. "Coke is it;" "Western Airlines — the only way to fly;" and "Seven-Up — the Uncola" are examples of tags.

If you are called on to do a tag, consider yourself blessed. You have a chance to make some quick, easy money. If you are union (we'll talk more about unions in Chapter Ten) and are hired for a full eight-hour session, you are obliged to be available for those eight hours of work. The producer is obliged to pay you scale (the established wage rate set forth in the contract between the union and the producer) for that session. But if you record the tag to the producer's satisfaction in anything less than eight hours, even if it's five minutes, you will be free to leave, and you will still be paid as if you had worked the full eight hours.

Tags are deliberately written to make a lasting impression on the listener. And that is how they should be delivered. Tags are always "punched," never "pushed" or "forced." Pitch may drop in a reading for dramatic effect, but not the energy or volume. We'll give you some tags to work on at the end of this Chapter.

Up to this point, we have kept the commercial voice-over focus on "singles" or one-person spots. Now it's time to consider "doubles," or two-person spots. The beginning of our Introduction to this book was much like a double, with both of us speaking as one person to you, the other person in the spot.

Since doubles are often done on radio or television but are seldom published in magazines, we will provide some two-person spots for you to study and use for practice.

Here's a double for the fictitious Bingham's Furniture Store.

NEPHEW:	Well, how do you like it?
AUNT:	This is your new apartment?
NEPHEW:	Well, it's new to me. It's my very first apartment.
AUNT:	There's a hot plate on top of the television set!
NEPHEW:	Yes. I call that my kitchen.
AUNT:	What's this? Oh, a walk-in closet.
NEPHEW:	That's the bathroom, Aunt Marian.
AUNT:	Oh, dear! Where's the bedroom?
NEPHEW:	You just sat down on it.
AUNT:	You sleep on the couch?
NEPHEW:	It's a queen-size sofa bed from Bingham's Furniture Store.
AUNT:	From Bingham's? Well, there's hope for this place after all!

Notice how, just like a single, the double is actually a miniature play. It has a beginning, a middle and an end: Aunt Marian comes into her nephew's new apartment; she starts discovering the features of the apartment and becomes more and more troubled by her findings; at last there is peace when Aunt Marian learns that her nephew is sleeping on a Bingham's sofa bed.

There is no "secret" to doing doubles. Treat them as you would a single — understand the copy, visualize it, become your character and deliver the lines. But remember this important difference between doubles and singles: In a double, you have the person to whom you are speaking actually standing right next to you. Since the dialogue is between the two of you, listen and react to what your partner's character says.

The very best acting really isn't "acting" at all — it's based on reality and what we do naturally, listening and reacting to other people. We suggest that you meet regularly with a few voice-artist friends to work on doubles and even multiples. You'll acquire skill in this area, plus you will give and get immediate feedback on your performances.

Always work with your partner as a fellow artist, too. On an audition, you may be competing for a job, but do not compete with your partner during the reading of your particular spot. The more the two of you cooperate and are mutually-supportive, the more you will enhance your own readings. Working doubles simply means that you are playing another game — one that can be contagiously exciting and a whole lot of fun. All you need is a partner who has an imagination and a willingness to play like a child — abandoning every inhibition and committing totally to a particular character.

Ask your partners how they "see" the copy. If your partners' feelings are in agreement with your own, your work is already half-done. If you have the time to do a quick run-through with your partners without disturbing anyone, do so. Step outside for privacy, if you want. If you don't have the time, or if your partners prefer not to do a run-through, just keep your character firmly in mind. Be ready to commit to that character and to your picture of the copy when the time comes to tape it. Remember, too, to listen to your partners, so you can at least react to them.

If your partners have no particular thoughts as to how a piece of copy should be read, describe your own visualization of what is going on in the text. The more clearly you paint the picture, the greater the chances your partners will see it too and be able to hold that same picture in mind when recording.

Sometimes your partners will have a completely different idea of what is going on. Always give them the courtesy of hearing them out. Perhaps they have thought of something that hadn't occurred to you — something that would make your readings terrific. But if you can't honestly agree with their concept, ask them if they would be willing to try it your way in a practice run-through. Sometimes other voice-over artists need to read copy a particular way in order to "hear it" and get a feel for it.

When you can't persuade your partners to do it your way and there is a great deal of resistance on their part, don't force the issue. This will only cause resentment and animosity, which will inevitably show up in your readings. A mike never lies.

Chances are difficult partners are not deliberately being difficult; they may have had a rough day, or they just may be arm-wrestling with a bad case of nerves. But don't risk picking up their negativity. Smile encouragingly, then move away to a place where you can keep your own positive energy intact. You can always ask the director for guidance once you get inside the studio.

When you do get in to record, don't be concerned if your partners give a poor performance. Your concern and worry will only use up the energy you need for your own reading. And even if your performance is up to its usual high standards, your partners' "off" readings will make yours sound that much better.

Remember basic mike techniques, too. In the unlikely event you are sharing a microphone, mike courtesy calls for you to do just that — share the mike. Only a nonprofessional hogs the microphone. Deliver your lines to your partner, but do not turn your head away from the mike to do so.

To make your doubles sound completely natural, use what people do in their everyday conversations. When one person speaks, the other reacts. Add sounds to the text, as audible reactions to what your partner is saying. A mike won't capture the skepticism of a raised eyebrow, but it will catch the "Hmmm" you can interject into a reading. Before one person completely finishes speaking, the other usually jumps right in and contributes his or her two cents to the conversation. Practice overlapping (but be careful not to "step on") lines, and watch out for long pauses, which will sabotage even the best readings with dead air.

Here are some more doubles for you to practice with a partner. Take turns doing the different parts, changing the text and/or the sex of any given speaker to accommodate your readings. Either one of you may be the Announcer; just remember, the Announcer is always another, completely different, character from the speakers.

(FROM OFF) means the line is to be said slightly to one side of or back from the mike so the speaker will seem to be in another location. (MOVING OFF) means the speaker is to deliver the line while moving away from the mike, thus indicating that he or she is leaving the room.

Tape all your readings, and give each other detailed, constructive criticism. Finally, enjoy the game. Have a ball starring in all sorts of mini-plays, endowing each piece of copy with its own very special life.

ROMANO'S PIZZA

CUSTOMER: I'd like a pizza, please.

SERVER: We got chicken and spareribs.

CUSTOMER: No, I'd really like a pizza.

SERVER: How about fish filets or a ham-
                 burger?

CUSTOMER: All I want is a pepperoni
                 pizza.

SERVER: Pork chops? Maybe a taco?

CUSTOMER: I thought this was a pizza
                 place.

SERVER: It is, but our specialty is va-
                 riety.

CUSTOMER: I don't want variety. I just
                 want a pizza!

SERVER: Oh.

ANNOUNCER: When you want a pizza — and
              nothing else will do — come to
              Romano's Pizza. We only do what
              we do best.

              BLU'S SHOE STORES

CLERK: I checked in the back and we
              don't have that shoe in your
              size. But I'm sure this one'll
              fit.

CUSTOMER: That's not the style I wanted.

CLERK: Well, we're out of that exact
              style, but this one's just like
              it.

CUSTOMER: No, it's not. It's not even the
              color I wanted.

CLERK: Red, blue — what's the differ-
              ence? Here, try it on.

CUSTOMER: I can't ... get my foot in.

CLERK: Push! Again! Harder!

CUSTOMER: Ouch!!!

CLERK: There you go. Look at that fit!

CUSTOMER: It's squashing my toes!

CLERK:	Snug. Just the way it should be.
CUSTOMER:	Take it off! It's killing me!
CLERK:	You're just not used to high fashion.
CUSTOMER:	I didn't want "high fashion" in the first place!
CLERK:	Well, make up your mind. Do you want style or do you want comfort?
ANNOUNCER:	If you want style and comfort, come to Blu's — where the shoe fits you.
CUSTOMER:	It's not coming off!
CLERK:	Pull harder!
CUSTOMER:	My toes! I can't feel my toes!

BUD MULLIN'S CANDY BARS

INTERVIEWER:	Hello. Today we're coming to you straight from the Zoo, where I'm talking with Ollie the Owl.
OLLIE:	I take it this is your standard P.R. interview: the usual questions about food, lodgings, and

so forth to impress the general public?

INTERVIEWER: That's right, Ollie. Just like last year.

OLLIE: Not just like last year.

INTERVIEWER: What do you mean?

OLLIE: Last year I did thirty minutes on "How I Love Living In The Zoo" and I never saw a single dime.

INTERVIEWER: Ollie, no one gets paid for doing these spots.

OLLIE: Was I good last year?

INTERVIEWER: You were the best.

OLLIE: And you want me to do your show again?

INTERVIEWER: Absolutely.

OLLIE: Then sign here.

INTERVIEWER: What's that?

OLLIE: My contract. It says I get paid in Bud Mullin's Candy Bars.

INTERVIEWER: Candy bars? But you're an owl!

OLLIE: An owl who got wise to the delicious, rich milk chocolate in

Bud Mullin's Candy Bars. Do we
have a deal or don't we?

INTERVIEWER: Ollie, I ....

OLLIE: No candy — no talkee!

INTERVIEWER: You win, Ollie.

OLLIE: My agent said I would.

CURRY'S DEPARTMENT STORE

SPEAKER #1:   I like your coat!

SPEAKER #2:   Thanks.

SPEAKER #1:   If I didn't know better, I'd
                say it was new.

SPEAKER #2:   It is new.

SPEAKER #1:   No!

SPEAKER #2:   Yes!

SPEAKER #1:   But you bought a new coat last
                year.

SPEAKER #2:   I buy a new coat every year.

SPEAKER #1:   Wait a minute. I know how much
                you make. How can you afford
                it?

SPEAKER #2:   I shop smart. I shop at Curry's.

ANNOUNCER: Curry's: Quality and style at
                  affordable prices.

                  WAGNER'S DOG FOOD

KID #1:   My dog Pepper is the very best
                  dog in the whole wide world.

KID #2:   Uh-uh. My dog's the best.

KID #1:   He is not!

KID #2:   Is, too!

KID #1:   Pepper's more happier than your
                  dog.

KID #2:   He is not!

KID #1:   Is so!

KID #2:   Oh, yeah?   How come?

KID #1:   'Cause I feed him Wagner's Dry
                  Dog Food.

KID #2:   Yeccch!

KID #1:   That's not what Pepper says.

ANNOUNCER: Wagner's Dry Dog Food — for the
                  "very best dogs in the whole
                  wide world."

BARBARA'S CHOCOLATE CHIP COOKIES

DAD: (FROM OFF) Davey?

DAVEY: Uh oh —

DAD: (FROM OFF) Where are you?

DAVEY: I'm ... in the kitchen, Dad.

DAD: (FROM OFF) What are you doing
            in there?

DAVEY: Nothing!

DAD: (FROM OFF) Are you eating cook-
            ies again?

DAVEY: Me?

DAD: (FROM OFF) Are you?

DAVEY: Nope! Uh-uh! No way!

DAD: (FROM OFF) Honest?

DAVEY: No.

DAD: (FROM OFF) When I tell your
            Mother what you've been up
            to...!

DAVEY: But Dad, these are Barbara's
            Chocolate Chip Cookies!

DAD: (FROM OFF) Barbara's Chocolate
                Chip Cookies? Uh, Davey, you'd
                better bring those cookies in
                here. I'll keep them under sur-
                veillance.

DAVEY: What does "under surveillance"
                mean?

DAD: (FROM OFF) It means "I won't
                tell your Mother what you've
                been up to if you bring me
                those Barbara's Chocolate Chip
                Cookies!"

                TUCKER'S LONG DISTANCE DIALING

DAUGHTER: Mom, can I call Freddie?

MOTHER: Is he the one who calls you col-
                lect?

DAUGHTER: No, that's Tommy.

MOTHER: I thought he was the one who
                wines and dines you — Dutch
                treat.

DAUGHTER: No, that's Bobby.

MOTHER: Isn't he the one who brings you
                his dirty laundry?

DAUGHTER: No, that's Richie.

MOTHER: I give up. Who's Freddie?

DAUGHTER: He's the one you like.

MOTHER: Oh, that Freddie! Well, by all
                   means, call him.

DAUGHTER: Thanks, Mom. I'll tell him you
                   miss him.

MOTHER: Miss him?

DAUGHTER: (MOVING OFF) Freddie just moved
                   to New York last week.

ANNOUNCER: Thank goodness for Tucker's
                   Long Distance Dialing — and for
                   all the Freddies in your life,
                   wherever they may be!

Exercises:

Read over the tags at the end of this chapter. Go through magazine ads and listen to radio and television commercials to choose tags you would like to work on — ones that feel like something the "natural you" would say. Practice delivering the tags as if each one contained the most important information about the very best product there is.

Now go back and get those tags that you passed up in the first exercise. Run through your list of characters and let each one record different tags. In playback, decide which character works saying which tag.

Keep notes on this; later you may wish to include a string of tags on your demo tape. We highly recommend that you do so; it is an excellent, quick way of showcasing your talent.

This exercise is designed for doubles, but it can also work for singles. It involves improvisation and is a terrific way for the nonactor to practice acting.

On individual slips of paper, write one or two lines to describe different people in different situations, then fold the papers and put them into a bowl or a box. Take turns drawing the slips one by one, become those characters and act out the situations described.

Here's an example: A man and wife, married for a long time, go shopping for a car they've wanted to buy for six months. Notice we did not put in a lot of details; always give just enough information so that you and your partner can make some choices and start a dialogue.

Once you have done a particular situation, put it back in the container. The next time you draw it, do it another way.

TAGS

Silhouettes by Joseph Bean. A cut above the rest.

Nadale's Nifty Neckware. Tie one on.

Who's calling? Andy's Message Service can answer that one.

Hamilton's Hardware. Always the best or you can nail us on it.

Sigman Opera Glasses. They're worth a look.

Yvonne's Heavenly Donuts. What a holy experience!

Steven's Underwear. Never leaves you in a bind.

Zubler's Zinfandel. When the occasion is so special, the wine must match it.

Sattin's Plant Care. Offers all sorts of growth opportunities.

Burnham's Books for Children. Tall tales for little people.

Cavanaugh's Bakery. Where you can have your cake and eat it, too.

Poole's Party Favors. For all your guests of honor.

Momma and Poppa B's Bingo Parlor. Are you game?

Zabala's Remodeling Service. We'll make your dream home come true.

McGowan's Typing Service. The keys to success.

Attention: Funny People! Bulen's Agency for Comedians. We'll put your career on the right laugh track.

Carver's Casino. Fun? You can bet on it!

Chapter Seven

The Demo Tape

Demo (demonstration) tapes are an expensive, but essential, tool of this trade. They are our calling cards, ways of introducing ourselves to casting directors or agents.

Because demos are so expensive to make (they range anywhere from $300 to $700 or more), they should not be cut until you are both good enough and ready to record one. Wait until you have mastered the Basic Process and supplementary techniques, and have developed a fairly large stable of believable characters before you pay good money for something that will not pay you back.

There is other homework you must do before you are truly ready to record a demo tape. You need to call various studios to compare recording rates and tape duplication costs. In Appendices B, C, and D, we've given the names of some of the people and companies providing demo tape production and duplication services, as well as graphics for your tape containers. Prices and quality do vary from one studio to the next. We suggest that you ask your teachers and other people in the business for their recommendations, then shop around.

Sometimes, if you can guarantee the booking of several people who are willing to record their tapes during one long session, you might be able to get a special group rate. Just make certain that each person knows he or she must stick to a predetermined length of time in which to record his or her tape.

Finally, you will need a script — one which you have carefully prepared and then practiced at home just the way you plan to record it in the studio.

The ideal length of a demo tape is based on the principle that "less is more." Characters should appear for no longer than the time it takes to establish them. This can range from the few words of a tag to a complete fifteen- or twenty-second commercial. The number of spots you do should correspond directly to the number of different, excellent and sustainable characters you do.

Generally, demo tapes should not run longer than two and one-half to three minutes. Kathy Levin, who works at Bob Lloyd's The Voicecaster in Los Angeles, stresses that agents and casting directors are innundated with demo tapes to which they can devote very little listening time.

Don't despair — it is possible to put together an outstanding, yet compact, demo that will knock their socks off. Pat Fraley did it. His arresting, unique character tape runs only one minute, yet he managed to put sixteen different voices on it!

It is up to you whether you use actual copy or create original material for your demo tape. There are pros and cons to both approaches.

In general, it is okay to use material that has been written and recorded by someone else for a real product or company — as long as your use of the material is for talent demonstration purposes only. Some people prefer prerecorded material and don't mind running the risk of being compared to the people who have already done the spots. They feel that familiar copy will focus their listeners' attention where it belongs — on the characters themselves and not on the copy. On the other hand, agents and casting directors do complain about hearing the "same old spots over and over again."

If you write your own copy (or have someone else write it for you), you can pleasantly surprise your listeners with fresh, new material that will hold their interest. However, good copy, while it is easy to recognize, is not always easy to write. Get several independent and objective opinions about the quality of your original material before you put it on your tape.

Voice-over artists often use a mixture of actual prerecorded material and original copy. We recommend that you use whatever best showcases your talents. Voice-over artist Jack Angel, former radio announcer with KMPC and KFI in Los Angeles, recommends that, as a beginner, you do the first spot on your demo tape in your own natural voice. This answers the question agents and casting directors always ask: "What does this person really sound like?" Once they have this point of reference, they are more apt to show interest in discovering your entire range of voices.

Stressing how little time professional listeners have to hear demo tapes, Jack urges you to "grab them within the first ten to fifteen seconds with a dynamite 'you' spot, or they will yank your tape out of their machines and go on to the next one."

Jack recommends that you follow this with commercials which won't "date" you. If you pick a spot that is several years old, casting people may recognize it and wonder whether all your material dates back to the Ice Age. Jack suggests that you include a variety of interesting voices on your tape. He cautions that the characters you do must be "ones you can quickly and easily go into and maintain on an audition or on a job."

What if you don't have a variety of interesting voices? If you have only one or two characters, but you do them extremely well, do them and don't try to pad your tape with voices that are less than excellent. It is better to do one minute of what you do well and impress your listeners, than to clutter your tape with unsuccessful attempts at variety and lose your appreciative audience.

Kathy Levin says: "It is most important that you only do what you do best on a demo. In other words, if you are a female and all you do are adult female voices, don't manufacture a baby voice just for the sake of variety. Variety within what you do best may actually be achieved by your choice of script."

Dona Lee Davies concurs, adding: "Even if all you have is one excellent voice, that voice can be convincingly altered by simply changing your attitude."

Vary your spots in terms of pacing, pitch, hard and soft sells, long and short copy. Never let your longer pieces run more than twenty seconds. A series of tags is a very good way to quickly showcase a variety of characters, but be careful not to duplicate a voice you have already used. As Jack Angel says, "At that point, the professional listener figures 'this is where I came in,' and moves on to the next person's tape."

Make certain your impressions are excellent. Kathy Levin complains that: "We frequently get tapes with sound-alikes on them and they are simply not competitive. If those people could hear Frank Welker do Gregory Peck, they would never put down a less-than-perfect impression of him again!" She adds: "We also get people who list numerous impressions they do — sometimes numbering up to 100 voices. Now, come on!"

There is disagreement in the industry as to whether or not you should include a double on your tape. Some professionals feel that a double is needed to prove that you can work well with another person. Others are concerned that your listeners may be more impressed with your partner's voice than with your own.

If you do opt to include a double, choose a partner of the opposite sex. Jack Angel tells of the time he put a double he had recorded with Alan Barzman on his demo tape. Someone in the industry heard the spot and called Jack in "on a rush." He dropped everything, jumped in his car and raced over to the audition. When he got there he learned, much to his embarrassment, that they wanted him to "do the voice that sounds like Alan Barzman."

A footnote to show just how crazy this business can be: Jack adds that as soon as he 'fessed up about Barzman's voice, the producers rushed to get Alan in to audition since they absolutely "had to have his voice." Alan auditioned for them ... and he did not get the job, either!

John Westmoreland cautions: "Even using a partner of the opposite sex is no guarantee that you will attract more attention than your partner. I've cast 'the other person' from people's demo tapes. Yet doubles are good because they demonstrate a certain sense of timing, and often show a comedic edge that won't come through in a single."

As your talent evolves, so should your demo tape. Jack Angel suggests that once you have a good, recognizable, professional commercial to your credit, you should begin your tape with that spot. New material can easily be cut into your master at any time to replace older spots, or you can record a whole new tape if you prefer.

We recommend that you consider your next move very carefully before taking action, because of the costs involved. Not only must you pay for all recording and/or editing time, but there is also the cost of having copies made to replace your old duplicates. You certainly don't need to spend money on a new tape that will end up sounding just like your old one. Our rule of thumb for making changes on your demo or for having a new tape made is: Don't do it unless you have reached a significant new level of growth, and you can afford the costs involved.

The demo tape represents you. In your absence, it auditions for you. Therefore, it should always showcase your very best work and be of the highest quality. When it is heard you will not be around to plead: "I could have done better if I'd had better copy;" or (our favorite) "The engineer is my brother-in-law, so I had to use him. Actually, he's not really an engineer, but he plans to go to school for it next year."

Once you choose the material for your demo and determine the order in which you want to present it, you need to select the music and sound effects you want to include. Go through your own music library. Listen for background music and sound effects that will complement and not detract from each spot by calling undue attention to themselves.

Don't discount the effects of using background music on your demo. In addition to establishing a particular mood, music greatly adds to the flow and dynamics of your production. It is a distinctive touch that will enhance the professionalism of your tape.

If you cannot find any suitable background music or sound effects, ask your fellow voice-over students or friends if they have anything you could use. If they come up empty-handed, call the engineer where you plan to record. Sometimes recording studios keep extensive libraries of music and sound effects.

When you choose which sounds go with which spots, put your material into script format (see below). A two- or three-page script is easier to handle than a number of loose pages, each containing one spot, plus the fewer pages decrease the chances of the mike picking up paper noise. Script format also allows you ample room to make notes on and mark up your own copy. When you go in to record, however, present a clean copy of the script to your engineer and to your director, if you are fortunate enough to have one. This enables them to "stay with you" during the process and to do the necessary editing more easily.

The following are examples of two types of demo scripts. The first one was written for a woman who wanted to showcase her commercial characters. The copy also has a very loose "through-line" or story which runs the length of the script.

The second script was written for a man. He wanted to demonstrate a few of his characters but also include some spokes work, as well as tags.

Where individual character names are so personal that they might not identify a particular voice for you, we have simply written-in the type of voice we mean. "SFX" indicates "sound effects" or "music." "... MUSIC — ESTABLISH" means we should hear a few bars of the specified music — just enough to establish a mood — before the character begins to speak. "THEN UNDER" means that the music is to continue while the next speaker does his or her spot, then it stops.

SFX: ANIMAL SOUNDS — ESTABLISH, THEN
                UNDER

WANDA: Hello. Wanda Wonder here at the
                Zoo. Today we're talking with
                Lyle the Lion.

LYLE: (FEROCIOUS GROWL)

WANDA: The very large lion. How're you
                doing, Lyle?

LYLE: *Comme çi, comme ça.*

WANDA: Could you be a little more spe-
                cific?

LYLE: No.

WANDA: Would you like to tell our
                friends about your life here in
                the Zoo?

LYLE: No.

WANDA: I knew this wouldn't work.
                Well, moving right along to the
                monkey's cage...Uh. Lyle? You
                have your paw on my shoulder.

LYLE: I know.

WANDA: Look, Lyle, I have to go now.
                I'll call you, okay? We'll do
                lunch.

LYLE: How about today?

WANDA:	What?
LYLE:	Lunch. Today.
WANDA:	Oh, gee, I'd love to, but I already...
LYLE:	(FEROCIOUS GROWL)
WANDA:	Today would be great! I'm starving!
LYLE:	You're a real doll, Wanda.
SFX:	MUSIC BOX PLAYING — ESTABLISH, THEN UNDER
MOTHER:	My daughter Lisa got a new doll for her birthday. She named her Jeannie. Lisa says Jeannie is her very best friend.
TEENAGER:	Mother, get real. Lisa's best friend is food. I mean, she practically lives in the refrigerator. I made this pie for Brian — he's this totally outrageous guy my parents can't stand — and Lisa ate the whole thing. She is, like, such a pain.
OLD WOMAN:	Pain? You don't know from pain until you have dentures. Each morning they go in and by noon they fall out. Usually in public.

```
SFX:              SANDPAPER SCRATCHING UNDER
                  BROOKLYN ACCENT:
                  Are you bothered by flaky fall-
                  out? Do you ever get the itch
                  for long-lasting relief? Try
                  new Flake-Off for problem dan-
                  druff, and scratch that itch
                  for good.

SFX:              SEXY MOOD MUSIC UNDER

FRENCH DIA-       "Good" is not enough when it
LECT:             comes to champagne. The French
                  know it must be the best or it
                  should never touch your lips.
                  And the best champagne is
                  Duval. Duval — le meilleur cham-
                  pagne du monde.

WITCH:            How about a nice French apple
                  pie, dearie? No? How can I cast
                  a spell if you won't cooperate?

SFX:              SAME MUSIC BOX PLAYING — ESTAB-
                  LISH, THEN UNDER

KID:              (CALLING) Mom, how do you spell
                  'broken'? I'm writing this note
                  to thank Uncle Al for my doll
                  Jeannie, and I want to tell him
                  all about her. And Mom? We're
                  all out of pies, cakes and cook-
                  ies!

SFX:              STING
```

The next script has no through-line. It is composed of separate, individual spots. Some people prefer using this type of script because they feel their audience's attention will be focused completely on the voices and not on following a story, especially if the copy consists of prerecorded material.

Although we have used fictitious company or product names in the following demo script, the material should give you an idea of what using actual copy would be like.

Also, we have deliberately left out any sound notations this time. As an exercise, try selecting appropriate music and sound effects for this script.

DAD: I'm a freelance writer. For
                years my kids kept telling me:
                "Dad, get a computer." And I
                kept telling them: "Every day I
                fight with editors and publish-
                ers. I don't need to fight a ma-
                chine, too." That was before my
                kids bought me a Tangerine com-
                puter. Now my work practically
                writes itself, thanks to my Tan-
                gerine computer!

ATTORNEY: When the IRS computer eats your
                tax refund, call us. When your
                poodle plows under your
                neighbor's Victory Garden, call
                us. When the diamond lasts for-
                ever but the marriage doesn't,
                call us. We're the law offices
                of Fold, Bend, Staple and Muti-
                late — and we understand.

COOL DUDE: My lady. Here I am again, wait-
                ing for her to put on her make-
                up. Right about now she's doing
                her eyes. But what she does to
                those eyes is sensational! I
                call it "magic." She says it's
                X Factor. Magic or X Factor?
                Maybe the X Factor is the

magic. Whatever it is, it's
worth waiting for!

OLD MAN: The people at College U. believe that learning never stops
— and it never stops being fun,
either. At College U. anyone
can take an extension class,
even me. Especially me — I'm
not about to stop having fun!

CONSTRUCTION   Out here nails get driven,
WORKER: pounded. In the course of a
day, your nails take a terrible
beating, too. But you can fight
back with Claw-Care. Put it on
before bed. Claw-Care takes the
night shift and works straight
through so you can wake up to
stronger, healthier nails. Claw-
Care — helps you build better
nails.

TAGS: Vera's Vegetable Oil — the only
way to fry.
Sadie's Swim Wear — it'll suit
you ... just fine.
Chevillac — it'll drive you ...
wild!
Knot's Shoelaces — they're fit
to be tied!
Heaven's Scent — when the pursuit is no longer trivial.

CRUISE DIREC- What's the best way to get from
TOR: L.A. to L.A.? Board a lux-
uriously comfortable Dreamboat

cruise ship in L.A. and sail
down the coast with us. Shop,
sun and explore the ports of
Xihuatanejo, Puerto Vallarta
and Acapulco. Then relax and
feast your way back home. Dreamboat Cruises. The best way to
get from L.A. to L.A.

IRISH DIALECT: Have you searched the world
over for a place you could go?
Far away from the bother, with
the feelings of home? Come to
Ireland this summer, where
you'll find yourself welcome.
Caed mille failtes to Ireland —
welcome to our home.

Once you have recorded your tape, what is the next step? Have duplicate copies (dupes) run off.

How many and what kind? There is no hard and fast rule as to how many cassette dupes you should have made and how many reel-to-reel. We have seen casting directors as well as agents ask specifically for one or the other. Some prefer the superior quality of the reel, while others like listening to cassettes in the car on their way to and from work.

If you plan to do a blanket mailing, cassettes are the less expensive way to go. Often you can get a break on the price of having your cassette or reel-to-reel tapes duplicated if the volume is large enough.

But if you want to be more selective and send out fewer tapes, call ahead and ask what your professional listeners would like to receive. If you have an agent (see Chapter Eight), he or she may make certain recommendations that will include adding or eliminating material, or changing the order of your spots — which means a whole new set of dupes will have to be made.

Determine how many tapes you'll be sending out, plus a few more to have on hand (to take with you on auditions and for those unexpected opportunities that will arise). Add one for your parents, then place your order.

Never, under any circumstances, submit your master tape to anyone. If it is lost or damaged, you must record (and pay for) a whole new tape. The master should always stay in your possession and be kept in a sturdy box in a cool, dry, safe place. Label the box as well as the tape with your name and recording date, and mark it "Master."

Your dupes should be stored (and submitted) in individual plastic containers (cassettes) or individual boxes (reel-to-reel). All dupes should carry labels with your name and phone number on them. We suggest that you neatly label all containers with the same information, in case they get separated from the tapes somewhere in the submission process. And the "somewhere" is never in your own home; it always happens in the office of a complete stranger who doesn't know you and who winds up filing your tape in the wastebasket. Dupes also should be kept in a cool, dry, safe place.

Never place your tapes (master or dupes) on top of anything magnetic, such as the stereo or a home computer. If the magnetic field of your tapes is disrupted, they will be erased.

How do you submit a tape? First, here's some advice from Bob Lloyd, of Bob Lloyd's The Voicecaster, regarding tape submission to casting people. (We will discuss contacting and submitting to agents in Chapter Eight.)

Bob's personal preference is that the voice-over artist's first step is not to phone him, but submit to him by mail a demo tape along with a cover letter. Allow any busy person to whom you submit your tape a reasonable amount of time to listen to it. A follow-up phone call may be in order, but Bob and many other casting people we talked to request that you first mail in your tape, and then let them contact you through your agent.

Now, how do you submit that tape? If you are mailing a demo, make sure it is adequately protected. The Post Office sells padded envelopes that are ideal for tape mailings. While you are at the Post Office, take a tape along with you and find out exactly how much the postage will be.

Whether you hand-deliver (usually by invitation only) or mail in a tape, include a self-addressed, stamped envelope (S.A.S.E.) if you would like the tape returned. This is a professional courtesy that is extended to the people who are taking their time to listen to your tape.

Even when you include an S.A.S.E., you may not always get your tape back. Out of all the tapes that Molly Ann has submitted with an S.A.S.E., only twenty-five percent of them have ever been returned. Some "professionals" just throw the tapes away when they finish with them. Submit your tapes anyway, fully expecting your listeners to be as professional as you are. That way you won't turn off the true professionals.

You may wish to include a cover letter along with your demo. If there is anything that will make you stand out from all the other people who are also submitting their tapes, now is the time to call attention to it. If you have already spoken to the agent on the phone, refer to it in your letter. If you attended the same school as the casting director, mention it. If you know the spouse of the casting director (and don't mind if the casting director knows it), use that.

We have included three sample cover letters. These are only starting points. Use your imagination to create your own distinctive attention-grabbers, and remember to keep your letters (like your tape), "short, sweet and super!"

```
                              Your street address
                              Your city, state, zip


                              The date

Ms. _____, Casting Director
Tremble, Tumble and Thimble Advertising Agency
Their street address
Their city, state, zip


Dear Ms. _____,

Last night I attended the annual school play at my alma
mater, Braintrust College. I noticed in the program
that you directed the show. I thoroughly enjoyed the
production — you did a great job!

I understand that you are also the casting director for
Tremble, Tumble and Thimble. I am a voice-over artist
and would appreciate your taking a moment to listen to
my tape (enclosed).

Thank you for your time and I'm looking forward to see-
ing the next play you direct!

                              Sincerely,

                              Your signature

                              Your name, typed
```

Since the format of the following letters remains the same, we have simply included the bodies of the letters. This next one is to an agent.

Dear Mr. _____,

Do you know me? Most people don't. That's why I always carry my demo tape with me. I never leave home without it. Don't leave your office without listening to it!

                         Sincerely

                         (and I mean that),

This next letter is also to an agent, but it is more conservative.

Dear Mrs. _____,

I am a voice-over artist and am seeking representation. I do straight and character voices, and have enclosed a copy of my demo tape for your consideration.

Also included is a self-addressed, stamped envelope for your convenience in returning the tape, or I may be reached by phone at _____.
Thank you.

                         Sincerely,

Our recommendations sound like a lot of tedious and unnecessary work, but it is this attention to detail that distinguishes the professional from the amateur. Show that you know how to handle all phases of the business — like a professional — and, amazingly enough, that's when people will start treating you like one.

Chapter Eight

The Agent

It is important to remember that an agent's roster of voice-over talent consists of more than just one client. If your agent represents twenty voice-over artists (and that's a very conservative number!), he or she can spend only five percent of his/her time promoting you. You, however, can spend one hundred percent of your time promoting you. Along with developing voice-over excellence, it is your responsibility to do everything you can to promote yourself. (See Chapter Nine.)

So why bother having an agent? Because independent producers and casting directors contact agents when they need voice-over talent.

Producer John Westmoreland says: "We had three shelves full of demo tapes. We didn't want them, and we weren't asked if we wanted them; people just sent them to us. Why we kept the tapes is beyond me. We didn't have the time to listen to them. When we were casting, we always called agents."

Agents then call in clients they feel are right for the job and record each one of them doing the same spot. A tape containing all those voices is sent to the casting people, who then select the artists they wish to audition.

Agents also send out copies of their clients' demos, and are subsequently contacted by the producers and casting directors who have heard an artist's demo or other work and would like to audition that person for a job. Agents coordinate the times of their clients' auditions with the client's other auditions and/or jobs.

But the agent's most important function is to negotiate. Agents are responsible for securing the best possible terms for their clients once they have been selected for a job. Occasionally, agencies will produce "house tapes." A house tape is actually a talent agency's demo. On it are a series of short spots taken from its clients' demos. The spots are usually separated into groups of male and female voices, and each one is preceded by the artist's name. House tapes are sent out to casting people all over the world. Sound great? Oh, it is — but be careful! When your agent asks if you would like to be included on the house tape, before you jump up and down and shout a happy "You bet!," find out whether you are expected to pay for this privilege. A respected colleague got the shock of her young life when a bill arrived from her agent's company requesting payment of $150.00 for having included her on their house tape.

We are not saying "don't do it" — it's an excellent promotional opportunity. Just be aware that the opportunity may have a price tag attached to it.

How do you get an agent? For the fortunate few who already have an agent for theatrical or on-camera commercial work, that agent may be willing to sign them up for voice-overs. The rest of us play the time-honored game of hide-and-seek to get agents. They hide; you seek.

"Getting" an agent begins with "finding" an agent. Where do those elusive people hide themselves? In phone books and entertainment directories. Take out your local phone book and locate the listings of talent agencies. (In Appendix E, we've provided a list of some of the voice-over agencies in various parts of the country.)

Before you start making phone calls, try to find out from another source — your teacher, friends in the business, trade papers or entertainment-industry directories — whether each agency is large or small. Does it have a separate, long-standing, or recently-created voice-over division?

Jack Angel recommends that a beginner go with a smaller agency or with a newly-established voice-over division within an existing agency. In both cases, the agents are more likely to be open to screening new talent. They also want to be successful, and discovering excellent new talent (that's you!) makes them look very good indeed.

Call the agencies you want to approach, ask the receptionist for the name of the person who represents voice-over talent and ask to speak to that agent. Whether you actually speak to the agent or get bogged down at a more clerical level, be brief and keep your tone courteous, positive and professional. Identify yourself and state your reason for calling. Ask if you may send in your demo tape. You may be told that the agency is not interested in taking on any more voice-over people at this time. If so, make a note to check back with them in one or two months. Write down the name of the person with whom you spoke — later, when you call back, you can address him or her by name and possibly score a few points.

When you do get the green light and are told to mail in your demo, double-check the complete address and the spelling of the name of the person to whose attention you will be submitting your tape. Agents change agencies, and agencies change addresses with a frequency that seems to alarm only people who are outside the business.

Draft a cover letter (see Chapter Seven), include an S.A.S.E. and mail in your tape promptly. Then what? Sit back and wait for an answer? Not on your life! Never stop with one agent who might be very busy and can't get to your tape for months. Always do multiple submissions.

After a reasonable amount of time — about two weeks — you may call to see if your tape arrived and if the agent has had a chance to listen to it. If the agent hasn't yet played your demo, check back in another two weeks. Always remain polite and professional; never demand to know when the agent will get to it.

Agent Arlene Thornton of Arlene Thornton and Associates says: "I don't mind people calling after a reasonable amount of time — two or three weeks — but calling too soon or too often turns me off."

If the agent has listened to your demo, you may be informed that you have been turned down. There can be any number of reasons for the rejection: the agency may have "a conflict," which means they already represent someone who sounds "just like you;" or they need someone with more of a range than you have; or they just found out they are moving (again!) and can't be bothered; or they just "aren't interested."

Whatever the reason, and whether or not you agree with it (or even believe it), do not take it personally. Remain professional and don't argue.

If an agent says no, but takes the time to offer you some constructive criticism, ask if you may check back with him or her in a few months to see if the situation has changed.

It also is possible to get an agent by first getting a job. How? Sometimes independent producers or advertising agencies have their own casting directors and will hire directly, without going through agents. Consult your local phone book or entertainment directory for the listings of independent producers and ad agencies, then call and ask the support staff (not the casting directors, according to the ones we interviewed) for some information.

Find out if and when they hire from the outside. Make sure you ask whether they hire union or non-union talent. If you are non-union, for example, and learn that certain people are firm about hiring only union (SAG or AFTRA), don't bother submitting your tape to those people. They will only remember you as someone who wasted their time. If you do get work, you will then have some credits to your name and a track record to point to, which can make agents more inclined to sit up and take notice.

Do you know people who already have agents? Would they be willing to call their agents and ask them to listen to your tape? If your friends say yes and their agents say yes, that commitment represents one small step for your career and one giant step for mankind.

When you do get an agent, what happens? You will sign a contract. Read and understand every word in that document before you sign it. If you have any questions about anything in the contract, ask them — before you sign it. If the agent cannot explain something to your satisfaction, run it by an attorney — again, before you sign.

The contract should include a "performance clause." Agents generally have ninety days within which they must get you work or the contract can be considered void if you notify the agency and your union(s) in writing.

But considering how busy agents can be, how little time they can devote to any one client, and how many other people are right behind you trying to find an agent, it is in your best interests to get out there and promote yourself.

Once you have a "deal in the making," step back and let your agent do the negotiating. We are not suggesting that you bury your head in the sand and relinquish control of this phase of your career. What we do recommend is that you stay informed but let the agent, who is a professional negotiator, be free to do his or her job — just as you should be free to do yours.

A final word about agents. It may be a lot of fun to jog or play tennis with your agent, but those are pleasant, unexpected and nonessential extras. The one "must" in any agent/client relationship is trust. You entrust your agent with a significant part of your career; you must be certain he or she will work in your best interests.

How do you know? Check on the agent's performance. Ask around; find out what other people's agents do for them. But be fair. Remember you are just one of your agent's many clients, and as such may reasonably expect to have only a small percentage of his or her time. Allowing for that, is the small percentage given, quality time? Are you being recommended for jobs? Are your demo tapes being sent out? Are you getting any auditions? How are your employment negotiations being handled?

In addition to the overt signs, trust your intuition. If there is any doubt in your mind that your agent does not have your best interests at heart, that doubt will affect your ability to perform. The part of you that is worrying and wondering will not be available to do voice-overs. And if you are operating at less than one hundred percent, you will deliver less than one hundred percent — which means you will fall short of your normal high standards of voice-over excellence.

Questions:

"What sort of voices do you like to hear on a demo tape?"

We asked Arlene Thornton.

"Whatever you do best. If possible, it should include a straight or spokes, a Mom or Dad, a double, character voices, promos or tags, and singing, if you're good at it. This is helpful in animation work. I also like to hear your different age ranges."

Casting director Samantha Paris says: "The main thing that impresses me is someone who cares enough about their career that they know what is appropriate to put on a demo tape. If someone's tape is unprofessional, it alerts me to the fact that they probably haven't had real training or else they just don't care enough to find out the rules of the game. I want to hear who they are. I don't want to finish listening to a string of characters and wonder who they are. I don't like really convoluted tapes. I want to know you can sustain a character longer than three or four seconds. It must be believeable. I want to hear good acting."

"I know someone who got an agent without having a demo tape. Do I really need one to get an agent?"

Arlene answers: "You can get an agent without first having a demo tape, but this is rare. I like to hear a tape before I decide whether or not to interview the person.

"I did interview and sign someone once who didn't have a tape, but he was referred to me by a client whose opinion I respect. Once the man came in, though, I gave him a very thorough audition to make sure he had professional-level talent.

"Whether or not you have a demo tape before you get an agent, you definitely will need a tape once you have an agent."

"What do agents look for in a voice-over artist?"

Rita Vennari, of Sutton, Barth and Vennari, Inc. says, "I look for talent with an instinct to interpret copy creatively and intelligently."

ICM (International Creative Management, Inc.) Agent Jeff Danis says, "The world of voice-overs is a complete contradiction, just as is the world of any art. The last thing we need is another announcer, and yet there's always room for another good one. But I mean a real good one.

"It's not just enough to be adequate. You have to be great at what you do to make any type of substantial living. A living that would keep yourself and a top agent interested.

"The ingredients to be 'great,' I feel, are voice quality, reading and interpretation ability of copy and equally important, a great attitude. For without a great attitude, everything else is worthless."

Arlene Thornton says, "I like someone who wants to do it right, someone who treats the business professionally. Recently, I heard a young woman's tape. She had very little experience in the business, but I gave her an interview anyway because she filled a gap. I didn't have anyone who sounded like her as a client.

"She came in and was very professional, very motivated. She laid down some copy for me, and I knew she could get work, so I signed her. The very next day she went out and bought a phone answer machine, a beeper, professional labels for her tapes, and made herself completely available for auditions. That's what I look for — people who have talent and who treat this business seriously and professionally."

" So I can get signed if I don't have a lot of experience. What if I'm nonunion?"

Arlene again: "Yes, I'll sign nonunion talent if they're very good. They'll get into a union soon anyway if they're really that good.

"Back to the question of experience for a moment. If you don't have a lot of experience and I give you an interview based on your tape, there are a few things I want to know. Such as, 'Have you taken any voice-over classes or workshops? If so, whose?' 'Have you gotten any work on your own or have you tried to get any?' I want to know if you're motivated. Have you been doing leg work on your own? Or have you just been sitting around, waiting to be discovered? Lazy, I don't need.

"Voice-over is not a part-time job. Sure, you need a survival job to eat and pay the rent until your career really takes off, but make it the kind of job you can leave any time to go on auditions. You must be totally dedicated and available."

"I heard agents are innundated with demo tapes. Do they really listen to them?"

"I do," says Arlene, "and I keep notes on every tape I listen to. You never know what you'll find.

"When you call for a yes or a no on your tape, ask the agent if he or she can offer you any suggestions for improving your work. You may get some valuable feedback as to what you're doing right and wrong."

"Now that I have an agent, how often should I call her?"

Arlene answers: "Whenever you have a legitimate question or concern. I don't want my clients agonizing over how quiet it is right now, and 'is it the whole town or is it me?' I do want to hear from my people, but I don't necessarily have the time to call them all. They have to use good judgment and call me when there is a real reason to pick up that phone."

"Does an agent mind if I call producers myself?"

Arlene doesn't.

"Just don't bug them. You need to have good instincts about this, because nothing will turn off producers or agents faster than someone who won't leave them alone. Even if they like your talent, they'll soon start to dislike you. And they don't hire people they don't like. There are many other nice, talented people out there they can hire."

Libby Westby of Special Artists Agency, Inc., says: "I find my relationships with my clients work best when we look at their career as a shared responsibility. I can try to open doors by getting copy into the office and sending them out to auditions, but so much of the leg work depends on how creative they wish to be in selling themselves."

Bob Lloyd, owner of The Voicecaster, "takes lunch" with client John B. Curtis.

Linda Kwan pulls a tape from the Voicecaster's extensive library.

Linda Kwan, Pam Predisik and Kathy Levin of the Voicecaster work the phones to call in talent for auditions.

Lea Vernon and Greg Callahan rehearse their lines for a "double."

Robert Morse picks up "sides".

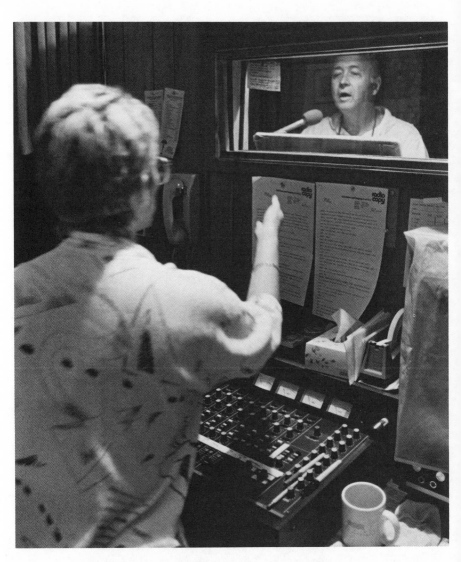

Kathy Levin at the controls recording voice-over artist Bob Ridgely.

Chapter Nine

Promoting Yourself

How should you promote yourself?

Any way you can!

In a business that is attracting more and more people, it is becoming increasingly difficult to "get in the door." Your voice-over excellence is certainly the key factor once you do get inside, but getting in — and staying there — can take lots of time and effort on your part.

Having contacts is an important means of promoting yourself. Knowing someone in the business can be most helpful in obtaining information as well as in making other contacts.

If you do know people already in the business, pump them for information. If they have no objections, tape your conversations with them. Why? There may be too much information for you to absorb at one time, especially if you are trying to think of other questions you would like to ask. Writing down your questions beforehand helps, but it doesn't allow for the unexpected twists, turns and tangents in an interview, which can provide a wealth of information you won't want to miss.

Taping a conversation also allows you to hear a professional's words again at a later date. Often, something that you simply glossed over will now JUMP OUT AT YOU. You hear it as if for the first time. And it may well be something you already know, but this time it has particular significance because it solves a problem you are facing at this moment.

If your contacts are well established in the business, ask them if you might accompany them on a job. Not only will you get a feel for a working voice-over environment, but you might also have an opportunity to meet casting directors. Don't impose on your contacts' time or intrude on their working schedules. Just be a sponge and absorb everything you can.

As Ginny McSwain says: "The seasoned pros are there for a reason. Their experience and successes have made them winners. They win parts or spots because they have a unique way of handling audition copy. They have a presence about them — it's evident in their interpretations."

For the beginner, watching professionals work is awesome and inspiring, especially when you understand how complex the whole process is — the process they make look so deceptively simple.

What if you don't know anyone in the business? How do you make contacts then?

Again, any way you can.

Socializing is a good way of promoting yourself and making contacts. In spite of all the work you do alone at home to gain voice-over excellence, the nature of our business is social. But you can't make contacts sitting at home waiting for them to come knocking on your door. Parties and gatherings of all kinds are choice places to meet people in the business. Get yourself invited to as many functions as possible.

Resumés are also important promotional tools. We recommend that you keep a professional, up-to-date resumé on hand to submit along with your demo or in place of it. Casting directors are already swamped with tapes, and when yours comes in, it will automatically be put on the bottom of the pile. A resumé may attract the attention of someone whose tired ears have "punched out," but whose eyes can still function. Also, from time to time we see ads in the trades (industry trade newspapers or magazines) specifically requesting that voice-over artists submit resumés instead of tapes for a particular job.

A beginner will normally have little, if any, experience to put on a resumé. Do one anyway, and list every related bit of information that might promote you. Make your resumé as distinctive and original as you wish, but keep it simple and easy to read.

Here are two samples. The first is that of an experienced female professional who has an agent. Under "Animation Experience," her cartoon credits are listed. Notice that she includes the names of the studios after the names of the shows.

T.H.E. PRO
CONTACT: A. Gent
Speak-Easy Voice-Over Agency
The Agent's Phone Number

SAG - AFTRA

CURRENT COMMERCIAL AND PROMOTIONAL EXPERIENCE:

This year's credits include:

- Curry's Department Store   (Local Radio)
- Barbara's Chocolate Chip Cookies   (National Radio)
- Wagner's Dog Food   (National Radio)
- Blu's Shoe Stores   (National Radio)
- Romano's Pizza   (Network Television)
- Tucker's Long Distance Dialing   (Network Television)
- Numerous Public Service Announcements   (National Cable)
- Fall Season Promotional Spots   (Network Television)

Complete list of this year's credits and lists of previous
years' credits available upon request.

CURRENT ANIMATION EXPERIENCE:

Current series include:

- Twitchy Witch; Casey-At-The Bat   (Boo's Cartoo's)
- Hummm Dinger; Wing-it   (The Spelling Bees)
- Ham Stir; Ms. Mouse The Grouse   (Rodent Revels)
- Chick Heard; Dawn Mare O'Dith   (Animal Olympics)
- Will O'Tree; Annie Oakley; Sick A'Mour   (Forest Frolicks)

List of past series credits available on request.

ACCENTS INCLUDE:

- Western American   - British   - French Canadian
- Bronx   - Parisian French   - Bavarian
- Brooklyn   - Russian   - Castilian
- Southern American - Australian   - Chinese

OTHER:

- Extensive A.D.R. experience

The second resume is for a male beginner who has no representation.

```
                         B. GINNER
                CONTACT: (Your phone number)
COMMERCIALS:
- Mullin's Small Curd Cottage Cheese              (Cable TV)


OTHER EXPERIENCE:

- Sports Announcer         (Braintrust College Radio Station)
- Public Service Announcer (Braintrust College Radio Station)


TRAINING:
- Susan Blu's Commercial Voice-Over Workshop
- Public Speaking and Debate                (Ona High School)


CHARACTERS:
- Father                      - Friendly Next Door Neighbor
- Child (4-5 years old)       - Not-so-friendly Policeman
- Child (9-10 years old)      - The Leprechaun
- Shy Teenager                - The Cowboy
- Outgoing "Surfer" Teenager  - Refined Southern Gentleman


IMPRESSIONS:

- James Cagney                - The Fonz
- Truman Capote               - Telly Savalas


ACCENTS:

- Bronx                       - Cockney



SPECIAL SKILLS:
- Fluent in Spanish
```

Another way to promote yourself is by using business cards. You can't always carry your demo tape or resumé around with you, nor is it always the right time to present them to a potential contact. Yet you never know when you will meet someone with whom you'd like to leave your name and phone number. Business cards provide a convenient, spontaneous way for the beginner to make a strong, professional impression.

Don't overlook the humble, old-fashioned thank-you note as a way of promoting yourself. Whenever you go on an audition or a job, or whenever a professional does you a favor, write a thank-you note. Not only is this common courtesy, but it also serves to put your name in front of those people one more time. And the more times they see your name, the greater the chances they will think of you when the next suitable job opportunity comes along.

Here are two examples of thank-you notes. The first one is to an agent who listened to your demo and turned you down, but who took the time to give you some constructive criticism.

```
Dear Mr. Gent,

Thank you for listening to my tape and for taking time
out of your busy day to give me some excellent sugges-
tions on how to improve my demo. I welcome and appreci-
ate your input. I do understand that you are not in a
position to take on any new clients at this time, but I
am holding the good thought that I soon will find an
agent as courteous and helpful as you have been.

Sincerely,
```

In the event you don't find another agent, that letter creates a nice impression, and it leaves the door open a little wider for you to call back and check with Mr. Gent at a later date.

The next note is to a casting director for whom you auditioned.

```
Dear Mrs. Hornsby,

Just a note to say "thanks" for giving me such a wonder-
ful opportunity to audition yesterday. From the moment
I walked in the door, you put me at ease and made the
entire experience thoroughly enjoyable.

Thank you for being so considerate.

Sincerely,
```

Stay informed. Read the trade papers. Split the cost of subscriptions with friends, if necessary, but as a well-informed voice-over artist, you definitely have the edge. You will become conversant with what is going on in the business and will be able to hold your own with anyone. You will also be in a position to seize opportunities as soon as they arise.

Jobs, of course, are often listed in the trades, but don't stop there. Really "get down" and read that paper so you become familiar with names in the business: voice-over artists, casting directors, ad agency executives, etc. Recognizing people's names and being able to comment on their latest accomplishments is an excellent way to please and to be remembered.

Keep up-to-date with movements in the business as well. If you are still looking for an agent or wish to change agents, by reading the trades you can often learn of agencies just starting up or of existing agencies announcing the "grand opening" of a voice-over division. Sometimes the new voice-over division turns out to be one overworked talent agent already on staff, who has just been given an additional title. But if the agency has hired or promoted or transferred sufficient staff to really accommodate voice-over artists, this is an excellent time to make contact.

How about a gimmick? Think of something within the boundaries of good taste that will amuse and attract attention. Some people have mailed out calendars with their names on them. Some send out key chains, fly swatters, letter openers, all with their names inscribed. Ideas don't have to be original, either. They can come from anywhere, and you can adapt them to your own needs.

At an early point in Jack Angel's career, he was working at a radio station in the San Francisco area. He wanted to get into voice-over work, and he got an idea for a promotional gimmick from one which had been used by the radio station. He sent out large "Jack Angel Loves You" Valentine posters to a number of advertisers in the area. The posters were beautifully done and carefully mailed in crushproof cylinders.

Jack followed them up a week later with his demo tape. When he went in person from one advertiser's office to the next to introduce himself, he found his face looking back at him from many office walls! He had made quite an impression, a much stronger one than if he had just phoned in to inquire about a job.

Instead of mailing out Christmas cards one year, Susan and her good friend Pat Fraley recorded a delightful Christmas tape which they sent to all their business contacts.

Be creative with your gimmicks. It is the unusual and unique that capture attention, so let your imagination really go wild when you are coming up with ideas for gimmicks. But when it comes time to implement one of your ideas, shift gears and be practical for a moment.

Ask yourself two questions: 1) Can your budget reasonably afford this planned madness? 2) Does your gimmick pass the good taste test? (This does not mean "Does it taste good?"!) If you get an unqualified yes to both questions, then pull out the stops and go for it!

Chapter Ten

The Audition

Congratulations! You finally have an audition! Acknowledge your success. After all, the fact that you were selected to audition is a success in itself. However, once the euphoria wears off, you may develop a horrendous case of nerves. Logic can tell you that worrying about the audition will not change its outcome and that worry is nothing more than a colossal waste of energy. But try telling that to the family of butterflies that has taken up residence in your stomach. Concentrate. Stay in the process, not in the panic, and approach the audition with professional commitment.

Make a note of the exact time, date and location of the audition. We suggest you put the information in a small calendar or notebook that you can carry around with you. In that same calendar or notebook, enter your mileage and any expenses incurred in going on the audition. The I.R.S. wants detailed records kept on deductible expenses, and you're much better off logging them in now than scrambling for them in the future.

When you get the call, you will probably be given only a brief description of what the spot will be, such as "a beer commercial." Rarely will you have a chance to look at any copy in advance, so concentrate on preparing yourself mentally and physically for the audition.

At home, run through the Loosening-Up Exercises you learned in Chapter One. As you dress, remember the "noise factor" caused by jewelry, loose change and certain fabrics. Stay away from perfumes or after-shave lotions. When you get nervous, they can become overpowering for you and for anyone else who has the misfortune of being trapped with you in a small studio.

Pack a briefcase to take with you. Borrow one if you have to, but the businesslike impression it creates is worth the trouble of getting one. Put two or three copies of your demo tape and resumé in the case. If the casting people have not heard your demo, ask after the audition if you might leave a copy with them. If you've already sent them your tape, it may have been misplaced. Plus ... you never know who else is going to be around that day.

Don't forget several sharpened pencils for marking the copy, and toss in a few of your business cards as well. Don't give one of your cards to the people who are expecting you; they already know who you are. The cards are for all the "you-never-know's" whom you might run into.

Before you walk out the door, choose something special you will treat yourself to after the audition. It doesn't have to be expensive; it can be as simple as feeding the ducks in the park or buying a Huey Lewis album. What makes it special is that it is a gift from you to you for a job well done.

Think as many positive, happy thoughts as you can to quiet those butterflies. Know that you know what you are doing. Get out of your own way, and let yourself be what you already are: an excellent voice-over artist.

Leave home in plenty of time to arrive at the audition fifteen to twenty minutes early. Allow time for traffic and finding a parking place.

On the way over, listen to music that will put you in the best frame of mind. Sing along with it to open yourself up. If you can't hold a tune, sing anyway — loudly. Also on the way over, do some Loosening-Up Exercises again.

When you arrive, remind yourself that you were invited to be there. The people inside truly wish you success; they want you to be the one they are looking for. Sign in and go over the copy using the Basic Process. Mark the copy as needed.

Now is the time to ask the director any questions you might have — such as how to pronounce the name of the product. Don't be unprofessional and take booth time to find out what you should have found out earlier. Casting directors often complain that many people don't seem to care; they just come in, read the copy, mispronounce the product's name, and have no idea what the product does. Show an interest; show you care. Also, ask what type of music they plan to mix in later, and keep the qualities of this sound in mind when you record.

A good way to build energy and loosen your mouth is to read the copy once or twice as fast as possible with no inflections whatsoever. Find a quiet, private place to do this and to practice your readings. Duck into the restroom, go out to your car, or just step outside the building for a few minutes, and get comfortable with that copy.

There will probably be an obvious choice and direction regarding the material. Naturally, go with the obvious or with the direction. But also be prepared to do the copy one or two other ways. Remember, don't stop with your decision to read it "softer" or "angrier." Run through the Basic Process and change your answers to one or more of the questions so that your readings will be believably different.

When you are called into the studio, introduce yourself to the casting director (if you haven't already done so), and shake hands. Be spontaneous and sincere in your greeting. Your natural charm and professionalism will win everyone over more quickly than your attempts to be witty and entertaining.

John Westmoreland has a classic "How Not To Impress A Casting Director" story.

"I was interviewing talent in a client's office. A young man came in. While he was waiting for me, he read the bulletin board. On it was some promotional information featuring an obscure song from the late Forties, a song I'd never heard of.

"But the guy knew the song. And when I went out to meet him, he greeted me with the entire lyrics to that song. I thought he was out of his mind. It wasn't my office; it wasn't my bulletin board; I had no idea what he was doing. Needless to say, he did not get the job."

Susan suggests that you "use the moment of introduction to memorize the names and faces of those involved in the casting process.

"I was out one day, and I ran into a very important client. He recognized me right away, but I had no idea who he was. He had to identify himself. It was embarrassing and certainly left a bad impression. From then on, I always made it a point to learn names and faces on all jobs and auditions."

So, that family of butterflies came along with you into the studio, did it? That's perfectly normal. The trick is to use those butterflies and make them work for you by turning "plain old nerves" into "positive energy." You know you're nervous and the casting people know you are, too, so don't waste time trying to conceal or suppress it. Take a deep breath and acknowledge the butterflies, then let them go and retain the energy as you exhale and focus on what you are about to do.

Place your copy on the stand and wait for the engineer to adjust the mike to your height. You will probably then be asked for "a level." Start reading your copy just the way you plan to read it for the real take — same volume, same inflections, etc. This is done so that the engineer can adjust the equipment to best record your voice.

Unless you are taping a double, you will be all alone in the studio, and "they" will be speaking to you over the talk-back from the control room. An interesting phenomenon is that the warm and friendly casting person you just met and shook hands with becomes a terrifying THEY when he/she goes behind the glass of the control room. Keep in mind that it's still the same person.

Okay, but who are all those other people in that booth? There may be more than one casting director, not to mention their assistants, the engineer, and some assorted advertising people, such as the copywriter(s), one or two vice-presidents with their assistants, and probably somebody's grandmother. Don't let the number of people in the control room throw off your concentration.

On one audition that included serious subject matter, Molly Ann almost burst out laughing whenever she looked up and saw the staggering number of people crammed into the tiny control room. When one person moved, they all had to move. They looked like a chorus line of sardines. It took every ounce of Molly Ann's concentration not to "lose it."

Why are all those people in there? You can't hear what they are saying, so you figure they're talking about you. That's when you start to wonder if your slip is showing or if your fly is open, and chewing your fingernails up to your armpits seems a comforting thing to do. Well, don't! Knock off those negatives.

Many of those people are there just to observe. Some really have a "say" in the hiring decision. But many others are focusing on the copy — not on you. Consultations go on and on about how to make the copy better. And there's a golden opportunity. If you can deliver a fresh or different reading that will solve their problems, you'll have saved the day and a few people's necks as well. Gratitude, champagne and jobs will flow your way.

When the mike levels have been adjusted, the director or engineer will slate your name. ("This is Susan Blu. Take One.") If you are asked to slate your own name, do so. Then take a brief pause to refocus on your picture of the copy, commit to it, and "let 'er rip!"

On your very first take, as well as on the first takes you do following any changes in choice or direction, go all out with the copy. A director can always bring you back to another level. But if you "start low," you create the impression that this is the best you can do, the most energy and enthusiasm you can possibly generate for the product. No one will ever know how much more you could have done.

Never listen to your own voice, and never let your mind start criticizing your work as you go along. If you stumble over a word, we suggest you stop and start all over again. If you keep going, you might carry the thought of the mistake with you through the rest of the copy and lose your concentration. Worse, you might not get a chance to do another take. So, take a deep and relaxing breath, know you can read that copy perfectly, refocus on your picture and go for it.

Once you have done your first take, the director may suggest certain changes in your delivery and ask you to read the copy again. Whether you are given very specific direction or whether all you get is a word, take a moment — and only a moment — to make the adjustment. If you've been practicing the Basic Process, that's all you will need. Which is fortunate: because that's all they will give you. Your time is their money.

Suppose you are given the direction: "Do it again and this time make it sexier." Trying to make your voice sexier is not enough. Don't change the voice — change your attitude and your picture of the copy. Imagine you have just "slipped into something more comfortable" and are about to tell a very special secret to someone you find irresistible. It is late in the evening, and you are totally relaxed and very intimate in front of the fireplace. Commit to that picture, and your reading will melt the mike.

You may get the cryptic direction: "Do it again and give me something else." Here's where one of the alternative choices you made when you first read the copy will come in handy. (If you would like to refresh your memory as to what you did on an earlier take, ask to have that take played back.)

If you receive no direction at all, speak up. Ask if you may do another reading. If they have the time, they will always let you do another take. Often they are grateful that you cared enough about the copy to figure out another way of doing it. Your approach on an additional take may strike them as just the fresh or different one they were hoping for.

One mark of a professional is the ability to take direction and work with it. Never, never, never argue with a director about doing the copy his/her particular way. Incorporate the direction into the process. With your mastery of that process, you should be able to deliver believable readings that include any direction.

Sometimes the direction can get a little confusing. On one audition, Molly Ann was asked to "make it lighter, but don't lose the heavy stuff. Punch it, but don't push it. It's a soft sell, but hit the product name. Warm up the copy, but you don't have to sleep with it. And remember to keep it natural, because this spot is real."

Susan's also heard some good ones: "Let's bring comedy to its knees!" "I don't know what I'm trying to say — act better!" "Somewhere between here and there is the truth." "Act faster!"

Act faster? Go figure.

You can ask for clarification when you are presented with confusing or conflicting instructions. You won't always get it. The best you can do is the best you can do. Never critique your work out loud. That is the director's job. Also, it can destroy the director's confidence in your talent, especially if he or she feels you have done a good reading. If you receive a compliment, say thank you and then — shut up!

Susan didn't always know when to shut up.

"It was early in my career and I was on an audition for a double. We'd done take after take, and finally the director told us: 'That was good. Now, hold a minute.' Well, we held much longer than a minute. After a while I started complaining to my partner: 'We've been here forever! What do they want? I don't think they like me.'

"And a disembodied voice said: 'Yes, we like you. We just need to shorten the commercial a bit.'

"My mike had been on the whole time and I didn't know it! I thought they turned them off when they weren't working with us."

Susan has come up with an effective antidote for the terror of those nail-chewing moments when the people in the control room are talking and shaking their heads — even after the director has told you that the readings were "great."

She used to think: "My readings were really awful. They just didn't have the heart to tell me. And now they can't wait to audition the next person." It finally hit her that, for all she knew, those people were simply talking about the crummy weather or complaining that they hadn't yet received their tax refunds.

From that day on, Susan always "hears their words in my head, and what they're saying is: 'Wow! What a terrific reading that was! I've never heard such a performance! I've never seen such talent!'" These words go beautifully with shaking heads.

Finally it's over. Miraculously, you have lived through it. Thank the people who gave you the audition, and leave on as positive a note as the one you came in on. Don't rush out the door like they're giving away free food down the block. On the other hand, don't linger any longer than politeness and necessity dictate.

Every now and then, as you walk out the door, the thought will hit you: "Now I know how I should have done it!" If you truly feel that this new reading is exactly what they are looking for, walk right back into that studio and politely ask if you might do it for them one more time.

Susan has done this on occasion, saying something like: "I have another approach you might like. Could I do it for you?" The worst they can say is "No, we don't want to hear it," and you will have lost nothing but a few moments of your time. Just be sure you can trust your feelings. We all get flashes of 20/20 hindsight about "how I could have done it better." Your feelings must be very strong and accurate in order to justify this request for a retake.

Once you make it to your car, climb in, roll up your windows and yell, scream, shout, laugh, cry. Release all those emotions that have been building up inside you.

You will probably think of at least two hundred better deliveries of your audition on the drive home. That's when the voice-over hangover begins: "They probably didn't like any of my readings. They would've told me if they did. All they said was, 'Thank you. Nice job.' They probably didn't mean that, either!" And it goes on and on and on — if you let it.

Second-guessing is self-defeating. There is no correlation between the praise you receive on an audition and getting the job. Susan swears that whenever she hears compliments — "That was a fabulous reading, just terrific," — she hasn't gotten the job. When all she hears is a lukewarm, barely audible "Uh, thanks," she gets the job every time.

So when you catch yourself whizzing down a negative mental slalom, put on the brakes and think about something else. Stay positive.

If you get a call-back, keep the same professionalism you had before, but don't try to recapture the identical audition. If you focus on the past, you leave no room for the wonderful creative spontaneity that got you the call-back in the first place.

Questions:

"What does a casting director look for in an audition?"

Samantha Paris says: "I'm looking for people who don't need their hand held, people who are professionals. I'm also looking for flexibility and versatility, people who can take direction and give me something completely different on take two. Most of all, I want someone who's willing to bring their own magic to a script. An audition situation can bring out a conservative approach in some actors because they are afraid to risk in front of a casting director. I try to impress upon people that I'm on their side. I want them to be really good because my reputation is on the line."

"I didn't get a call-back. What do I do?"

Jack Angel emphasizes if you don't get a job from an audition, don't feel that all is lost or that you've lost. Jack says the odds are you'll get one out of every ten jobs you audition for. Think of it this way: Each job you don't get brings you that much closer to the one you will get. When you do get a job, you're being paid for all those other auditions.

John Westmoreland says: "Casting is not infallible. Take your career seriously, but not the rejections. And don't get discouraged. It may not be you; casting is often done for the wrong reasons.

"There was an actor once who did the on-camera spots for a particular product. They gave him a special hat to wear and he looked terrific. He came across as a dignified, warm spokes with a good sense of humor.

"When it came time to do radio spots for the product, they automatically cast this man without making him audition. They should have. He was not a trained voice actor, and he did not know how to take voice-over direction."

John adds that "casting can be ridiculous because often there's no one person in charge. Everyone from the client's spouse to the janitor tosses in an opinion.

"Also there have been times when I've been asked to play house tapes over the phone for clients. It's foolish to cast people just because they sound good on a tape machine heard over a long-distance line, but it's done."

Susan says, "One company I'd been the spokes for suddenly decided it was time to do a new campaign with new talent. They put out a call for 'someone who sounds just like Susan Blu,' but they didn't want the real Susan Blu. I couldn't understand it; we'd had an excellent relationship over the years, but they just wouldn't see me.

"Finally, the casting director and I cooked up a scheme. I auditioned under another name just to see what would happen. I used the same voice I'd used on all their spots. When they heard that voice, they wanted it — over fifty others. Of course, then we had to tell them the truth.

"They took it well and they hired me. It was risky, though. They could have been angry and never hired me again."

"Is there anything 'special' I can do to impress casting people?"

Ginny McSwain says that "talent (especially multiple talents) always impresses me, but personalities and dispositions impress me, too. People who are open-minded enough to take direction, are open to new ideas, and know how to take risks and chances always score points with me. I also like people who are excellent readers and who know how to familiarize themselves instantly with 'cold copy.' What turns me off are people with bad attitudes. It's not hard to hear the 'edge' in a vocal performance when the talent is unfocused or has a bad attitude."

John Westmoreland told us, "Often it is the cute or unusual line reading that will stand out because no one has heard it before. And it can get you the job."

Susan confirms this with her "delicious" story. "The only line I had for this particular audition was 'It's delicious!' I read it a few different ways; they thanked me and said good-by. As I walked out the door, I tossed a very character 'Ooooh, it's delicious' over my shoulder. I was kidding, but the producer yelled: 'Wait a minute! Get back in here and do that again. That's the one we want!'

"Again, on another audition, I was halfway out the door when I called out in a character voice — 'Bye! See you later.' They hired me to do that voice."

"Are auditions seasonal?"

Commercial auditions often are. In sunny Southern California, there is a flurry of audition activity in late summer and around Christmas time. Why? Baby, it's cold outside! Advertising executives take refuge out here from the chilly New York and Chicago weather at those times of the year.

"Are auditions (and jobs) regional?"

Most voice-over work is done in the "major markets" such as New York, Chicago and Los Angeles. But don't discount local markets (called "units") for launching your voice-over career. It is often easier to get a few credits by doing some spots for a local radio station. The competition is not as fierce as it is in the major markets, and you may get into a union more quickly this way.

Samantha Paris, who casts in the San Francisco area, says: "The smaller market actor must be well versed in all types of voice-over, able to switch gears and understand the style of promos, comedic dialogue, narration and commercial characters. There's just not enough work available to specialize. Of course, the bottom line about working in voice-over is simple: If you are good, you will work. Actors come up with a lot of excuses for why they aren't working, but in all truth, excellence always finds an audience."

"Do I have to belong to a union to get a job?"

Not necessarily, and certainly not at the very beginning of your career. Nonunion jobs do exist, but they are generally fewer in number, harder to find, and less lucrative. Many producers have formal agreements with SAG (Screen Actors Guild) and/or AFTRA (American Federation of Television and Radio Artists), the two major unions which represent voice-over artists. As a union signatory, a producer must hire that union's talent.

That's great for voice-over students who are already guild members through other industry activities, but what about the person who belongs to neither union?

At the time of this printing, you can simply walk in off the street, pay an initiation fee and join AFTRA. SAG will not allow you to do this. You must be hired by a SAG-signatory producer for a union job. A producer can hire outside the union, but the paperwork involved usually discourages this practice. Many voice-over artists who are available for work are already guild members.

If you are hired for a union job, you have thirty days from the date of that first job to do as much union work as you can get, but after that thirty-day period, you must either become a member of SAG, or stop accepting union assignments. The union initiation fees (which can be rather steep), and the subsequent dues may seem a financial burden, but the benefits, credibility, and protection a union offers are the best bargains in town.

Chapter Eleven

Your First Job

Y ou've been waiting and waiting and waiting to hear whether or not you got the job. You don't dare call your agent — again. Just when you think you can stand it no longer, the phone rings and — "Congratulations! You got the job." Make certain you have the correct date, time and location of the job. Log it in your calendar or notebook.

The Big Day arrives, and there's an International Butterfly Convention taking place in your stomach. What to do? Basically, the same things you did for your audition. Eat something light. Take a relaxing bath or shower. Go through your Loosening-Up Exercises. When you dress, avoid noisemakers, strong perfumes and after-shaves.

If your voice starts to get thick (nerves can produce excess mucus), either suck on a lemon or sip hot tea with lemon in it. If you have a sore throat, a spoonful of honey or hot tea with honey will help. Stay away from dairy products — they induce mucus.

When your mind starts telling you, "You're going to forget everything you ever learned and fall flat on your face," replace that nasty little voice with the thought: "I had what it takes to get this job — I have what it takes to do it."

Leave home in plenty of time to arrive fifteen to twenty minutes early, just as you would for an audition. Make sure the director knows you are there. Get a copy of your script and find a nice, quiet place to go through the Basic Process and prepare for the reading. If you are working with another person, now is the time to introduce yourself and discuss your individual opinions on how the copy should be read.

When you are called in to record, remember to focus your energy on the material, visualize the copy and commit to your picture of it. You may, although this is rare, have a "buy" on the first take and be told you are free to leave. If so, you will have made a lot of money for a short day's work. But even if your first take turns out to be the buy, the director will usually want a few more done for back-up protection — a variety of takes from which to choose the very best one.

Usually, you will not be kept much longer than an hour for a commercial voice-over. The producers are paying for their time in the studio, and they want to move on to the editing process as quickly as possible.

Occasionally you will have to do take after take after take. Sometimes the ad people are not in agreement. They will often make changes up to and including the last minute. So don't blame yourself for frowns and huddled conversations in the control room.

If it looks like you are going to be in the studio for a long while, conserve your energy; ask for a stool to sit on. Make a quick trip to the restroom. Do a few stretching exercises to restore waning energy. Keep a cup of water handy; you'll need it to keep your mouth from drying up. There will be times when nothing seems to go right. You can't hit on a reading that pleases everybody. Time goes by. Then you give a great reading, but there is a technical foul-up. More time goes by. Then everything is technically perfect, but you flub a line. The ad people start huddling again and shaking their heads.

Just when you feel like you might as well move all your belongings into the studio and notify the post office of your change of address, you will be asked to "do it again — the way you did it the first time."

Don't fall apart! Stay loose, but keep up your terrific concentration. If you can't remember how you did Take One, ask the engineer to play back your first take. Because your readings evoke clear visual images, you will immediately know which picture you used for Take One and you can easily get back into it. (And it's probably the take they'll buy, too.)

No matter what happens, don't lose your sense of humor. Often you can defuse a tense situation with a humorous word; sometimes all it takes is a smile.

What if you get stuck working with an extremely difficult director? All we can say is that it does happen, but fortunately, very rarely. When it does, don't let the pressure get to you, and don't lose your professionalism. John Westmoreland worked with a particularly obnoxious director on commercials for a traveling arena show.

"A star had been cast for the production, but the director didn't like her, trust her, or want her in 'his' show. And he certainly didn't want her to do the commercials for it. The director (who was also directing the commercials) brought in his current no-name 'pet' for the TV and radio ads. The director was a very unpleasant, combative man. I spent fifteen minutes in the reception room with him, not knowing who he was. While we waited for the studio to be available, he wouldn't talk to anyone. He wasn't interested in associating with the agency, the star, or the production staff. With just a show of temperament, the star could have easily talked herself out of the whole tour. But she didn't. She had incredible self-discipline and professionalism, and her terrific attitude got her through that difficult time. And, ultimately, it paid off for her."

It's not always the director who tests your mettle. A friend of Susan's did at least fifty takes at one session. Everyone loved his readings except the writer, who kept saying "It's not right!" after each take. Finally they asked the writer to explain specifically what wasn't right. "It's just not me!" was his complaint.

Your goal is to be remembered as a professional, someone who is pleasant and cooperative to work with.

John Westmoreland remembers one actor who stayed pleasant and cooperative throughout a nightmare of a session. "He was supposed to be talking excitedly, over lots of traffic noise. We started in the studio and tried to energize him, but he sounded too controlled. He tried and tried, but he just couldn't get it. He was the spokes for the particular product being advertised, so we had to use him. We didn't really want to call in someone else because he'd always performed well before, but this time he was having difficulty with the copy.

"We wanted that slightly hysterical edge that comes from having taxis narrowly miss you. So we ended up putting him on a traffic island between two very busy streets. We ran the cable through the crosswalk and gaffed it to the street. I was standing on the sidewalk, four car-widths away, giving him hand signals. We got hysteria.

"We also got spots that could not be cut, because the sound effects were too heavy to match. So, not only did he have to give us excitement, he also had to be letter-perfect from beginning to end, and his timing had to be exact. He was a good actor and he did his best. All day. No complaints, no temper. His attitude made all the difference."

On your way out, remember to again thank the people you worked with. When you get home, write the producers a thank-you note. This thoughtful gesture serves to put your name in front of the "powers that be" one more time. Also, you may ask to have a copy of your spot mailed to your agent for inclusion on your demo.

Questions:

"When do I get paid for doing a job?"

If you do a nonunion job, you often will be paid immediately after the taping.

If you are union, the producers are required to send out your check within twelve working days of your employment. However, by the time your agent takes out his or her ten percent and sends you a check for the balance, the entire process can take anywhere from three to five weeks. If an ad agency cancels a session, for whatever reason, the talent must still be paid.

There is always the "other form of payment," which money can't buy: the thrill of hearing your spot on the radio or watching it on television. There's no way to put a dollar value on this one — it is such an incredible high!

"What are 'buyouts'?"

Arlene Thornton fielded this one.

"Complete buyouts (a flat, one-time fee paid for voice-over services) don't exist in union situations. Except for industrial narrations. Those are buyouts. Often, so is nonunion work. But where the talent is union and identifiable (as opposed to hand models, for example), payments and residuals go in thirteen-week cycles."

"Are jobs seasonal?"

John Westmoreland answers: "They can be. But it's not really fair to expect the production company to produce a spot in the season for which it is intended. We need a reasonable amount of lead time to prepare for the session. On the other hand, if you record far in advance of the target season, you aren't being fair to talent either, because you must put a hold on them. They are paid not to record copy for a competing product until their spots are run. But then you're paying actors not to do what they really want to do — act."

Chapter Twelve

A Few Final Thoughts

Or

"Out Of The Blu" & "Mullin' It Over"

Voice-over success is attainable; voice-over techniques can be learned and success can be achieved.

Ginny McSwain tells us that "voice-over is an art form unto itself. It is a craft that can and must be learned, just as on-camera techniques must be acquired. To succeed, professional actors must train to do voice-overs, just as fresh or 'green' talent must also train. Training, plus desire and commitment, will result in success."

Realistically, there will be times when you won't get the job. There may even be long stretches of time when you won't get any jobs. Voice-over artist Paul Kirby holds onto one thought after each turn-down: "It's all just a matter of selection, not rejection."

That thought helps ease the pain during those long dry spells. The one job you do get is the payoff for all the preparations you have done and all the auditions you have gone on.

As writer/producer Larry Belling says: "An attribute required by successful voice talents is a very thick skin. We know several pretty good voices who have auditioned over a thousand times and not landed one job. The competition is fierce!"

Don't let the frustrations end the game for you. As Director Andrea Romano states, "You must have the stamina to keep knocking on those doors!"

Be positive. Doubts have a sneaky way of creeping up on you at the worst possible times. These times correspond to your weakest and, therefore, most vulnerable moments.

One technique we use to stay positive is visualization. If you have mastered this technique for doing voice-overs, you will have a headstart in using it this particular way. When you get a call for an audition, picture yourself actually going on the audition. See yourself getting ready for it and going through all the preparations we discussed. See yourself driving to the audition, arriving, signing in and going over your copy. Imagine yourself doing an excellent reading of the copy and getting the job. If you can see something happening, you accept the possibility that it could happen.

Gordon Hunt, former casting director for the Mark Taper Forum and current director of recording for Hanna-Barbera, discusses fear in his book, HOW TO AUDITION. Although he only briefly touches on voice-over auditions, Gordon's extensive treatment of audition fears is well worth reading.

Don't downplay the importance of learning acting techniques regarding voice-overs.

Ginny McSwain's opinion: "Acting comes first, the voice comes second, and then the acquired technique for voice-over ties the two elements together. People who merely mimic, do impressions or make funny sounds must be able to sustain one or more characters throughout an entire script. Stand-up comics who are not actors have a great deal of trouble staying in character for any length of time; they are more used to a spontaneous, rapid-fire delivery for a limited period of time."

"Acting is very important," says John Westmoreland, "and in slice-of-life spots that require you to sound natural, you must lose the 'polish' that often comes with certain kinds of stage or on-camera training. A good acting class will give you the proper techniques without the artificial polish."

Always give credit where credit is due. Acknowledge those who have helped you, but don't forget to congratulate yourself on each step you take up the ladder. Recognition may come from others, but it means so much more if it comes to you from you. Only you know all the hours of work and sacrifices you made to become an excellent artist. It was your discipline, your efforts and your talent which made it happen. Respect yourself and your talent.

Casting director John Westmoreland has a healthy respect for voice-over actors because, "I did a free political spot once, and it really struck me what talent is paid for — their professional training. My nerves made my throat constrict, and my voice kept getting higher. You get what you pay for."

As you move up in the ever-widening circle of voice-over professionals, you will have the pleasure of meeting some of the most generous and giving people in the whole world. We have quoted a number of them in this book; others may be heard on the WORD OF MOUTH audiocassette tape. They are the first to celebrate your successes, and will gladly share their experience and tips with you. Secure in the knowledge of their own excellence, they have no need to distance themselves from "the competition," whom they regard as friends and colleagues in the business.

What makes a "winning" voice-over artist?

We asked several prominent voice-over artists for their insights, among them B. J. Ward: "I try to do everything I can to test my limits. Seasons of summer stock — doing a show each night, rehearsing another play during the day, with children's theatre on the weekend. Improvisational training and theater. Letting myself go on stage with no planned script and playing the improv games. Trusting myself and my fellow actors.

"Singing lessons. Learning my vocal range and strengths, how dependable an instrument I had, or have. (It's an on-going process).

"Voice-over workshops. Learning to work with my voice, reading lots of copy, getting the words up off the paper, making them mine and making my choices quickly.

"I learned a tremendous amount teaching voice-overs. Doing 'stand-up' and my own night club act. It all helps define who you are and what it is YOU have to offer. It helps to have a little talent and some good fortune. And while you're waiting...Be Happy. Appreciate what you have at any given moment. BE FUN TO BE AROUND."

Jennifer Darling: "The 'voice' is the major part of the whole mechanism that enables the actor to express herself. So I figured I'd better deal with it -

'the voice' - and once I did, I realized what a gift my voice was. I started dancing at the age of three, acting lessons at ten - and singing - imitating singers and doing dialects at eight. At fourteen I had a problematic appendectomy and had to stop dancing for a bit. I got very involved with singing, then went to New York to cut a record and appeared on the Ted Mack Amateur Hour and won. From then on, my voice became the center of my attention - I knew it was unique and would always help me to 'win.' At Carnegie Mellon University, I majored in Drama and also studied every aspect of the voice from dialects to Shakespeare. I toured the country doing repertory and found myself in New York where I appeared 'on' and 'off' Broadway for seven years doing Shakespeare for Joseph Papp, appearing in television for the David Frost Comedy Hour and also doing a soap opera; always working, studying, watching, listening and hopefully learning. When I came to California I got involved with 'nighttime' television. This was a new challenge for me and of course 'the voice' - a medium that deals with confinement and economy.

"TV and radio voice-overs were always fascinating, but then came animation. I could dig down deep and find all the characters that were lurking about. I could try them, stretch myself in another new way and get back to the beginnings of the theater and then some...and not be carried away for it. Here was another medium; all those artists sitting behind microphones doing a play; an outrageous play. I found yet another home, a new home in which to create. The world of animation; the voice knows no limits there. Trust yourself, study, follow your instincts and know that you are unique - listen to your inner voice so that you can win with your outer voice."

Dick Gautier: "I'm fortunate in that I divide my time between TV, movies, stage and the field of voice-overs and animation. When I was in my early 20s, before going 'legitimate,' I was a stand-up comedian whose stock and trade was weird sounds, offbeat impressions and various dialects. These strange talents lay dormant while I pursued film and TV roles, but when the world of animation and voice-overs beckoned, I quickly resuscitated the voices and dialects and now I'm having a terrific time doing voices for heavies, heroes and a host of bizarre creatures."

Linda Gary: "I have been an actress since I was a child, but I have only concentrated on voice-overs (commercial, theatrical, and cartoon) for the past twelve years. My achievement has mainly been due to my determination to 'be better,' to work hard, and enjoy that work. If I had to list my beliefs in what helped me attain whatever success I have achieved, I would have to say: Pay attention to the business acumen of being an actor, acknowledge those who help you along the way, maintain a professional attitude, be courteous to your fellow actors, listen to the director and be able to change instantly when the direction changes, don't rest on your past characters — create new ones (the car is a great place to create), don't whine, don't nag, and have fun!"

If the Basic Process and other techniques you learned in this book work for you, then don't abandon them when the going gets easy. They worked for you in the past, and they will continue to work for you in the future.

Never lose sight of the fact that voice-over is, as Brian Cummings says, the process of "becoming." Every piece of copy offers you the opportunity to use your creative energy to become a unique and different speaker for a particular product.

Voice-over is also "the process of becoming" in the sense that you must keep nurturing your talent if you wish to continue to improve and grow. If, at some point, you feel you have learned or have done it all, your talent will begin to stagnate.

Ginny McSwain feels that on-going, constructive workshops are an excellent place to nurture your talent. "Workshops provide a vocal work-out, using a variety of exercises. You don't just learn 'Voice-Over 101' and then 'have it.' The best workshops and classes push the artist to grow and to learn how to compete and how to win jobs. Workshops with guest speakers who are established in some area of the voice-over field allow you to get a feel for 'what's out there,' plus learn invaluable information from the speakers' own experiences."

So, continue to study and to practice, be persistant, and above all, be positive!

And now it's time for you to put this book down and concentrate on internalizing the entire voice-over process, so that all the techniques we discussed become second nature to you. With enough practice and repetition, voice-over excellence will become yours — instinctively and naturally.

Remember: The only limits you'll experience are the ones you place on yourself. And you have our sincerest and best wishes for unlimited success!

Appendices

The following voice-over workshops, private instruction classes and agencies, demo tape production, duplication and graphics services are included for your convenience. We simply found them by reading ads in the trades, nosing around in a few phone books and keeping our ears open; we do not necessarily endorse them. Likewise, the list is not comprehensive, and the fact that we may have omitted a particular person or company that provides any of the above services should not be construed as a mark against them.

APPENDIX A

WORKSHOPS/PRIVATE INSTRUCTION

Telephone these teachers to find those whose methods and approach best meet your own needs. Some teachers specialize in animation workshops, and may sometimes conduct general or commercial classes as well.

Chicago:

The Audition Studio (Hanna Dworkin)	(312) 527-4566
Audio One (Kirk Johnson, Sr.)	(312) 337-5111

Los Angeles:

Cindy Akers (Voicetrax West)	(213) 850-1112
Wally Burr	(818) 845-0500
Bob Bergen (Animation V/O Class)	(818) 901-8714
SUSAN BLU	(818) 501-1258
Louise Chamis	(818) 985-0130
Elaine Craig	(213) 469-8773
Dave & Dave (Dave S. Williams)	(213) 960-7833
Jennifer Darling	(818) 990-2270
Del Mar Media Arts (Bud Barth)	(714) 753-0570
Dolores Diehl (Voiceover Connections, Inc.)	(213) 384-9251
Pat Fraley	(818) 760-2748
Joanie Gerber	(213) 654-1159
Patty Glick	(310) 277-7247
Lou Hunt	(818) 763-4260
Ted Richards c/o Film Industry Workshops, Inc.	(818) 769-4146
Natalie C. O'Hare	(310) 454-9559
Nova Productions (Nick Omana)	(213) 969-0949
Stu Rosen	(213) 851-1661
Sounds Great (ADR) (Joan Ryan)	(818) 766-2808
Tobias Communications (Marice Tobias)	(213) 939-8679
Voices Voicecasting (Mary Lynn Wissner)	(818) 980-5659
The Voicecaster (Bob Lloyd)	(818) 841-5300

New York:

Madelyn Burns Seminar, Inc.	(212) 627-8880
Steve Harris' The Art of Voice	(212) 517-8616
Glen Holtzer	(212) 724-2800
Liz Noone	(410) 263-6040
VoiceWorks (Steve Garrin)	(212) 541-6592
Voiceovers Unlimited (Dan Duckworth)	1-800-888-VEOH
David Zema	(212) 473-3898

San Francisco:

Voice Factory (Taylor Korobow)	(415) 296-7753
VoiceTrax, San Francisco (S. Paris)	(415) 331-8800

Washington, DC/Baltimore/Philadelphia:

Liz Noone	(410) 263-6040
VoiceWorks (Steve Garrin)	(212) 541-6592

APPENDIX B

DEMO TAPE PRODUCTION

Chicago:

Chicago Recording Company (Hank Newberger)	(312) 822-9333
Audio One (Kirk Johnson, Sr.)	(312) 337-5111

Los Angeles:

Louise Chamis	(818) 985-0130
Michael Hamilton	(213) 466-7371
Lou Hunt	(818) 763-4260
Nova Productions (Nick Omana)	(213) 969-0949
Del Mar Media Arts (Bud Barth)	(714) 753-0570
Kris Stevens Enterprises	(818) 225-7585
Tobias Communications (Marice Tobias)	(213) 939-8679
Voices Voicecasting (Mary Lynn Wissner)	(818) 980-5659
Voicetrax West (Cindy Akers/Susan Palyo)	(213) 850-1112
The Voicecaster (Bob Lloyd)	(818) 841-5300

New York:

A & J Recording Studio (Gerald Kornbluth)	(212) 247-4860
Full House Productions (Jeff Bush)	(212) 645-2228
Steve Harris' The Art of Voice	(212) 517-8616
Glen Holtzer	(212) 724-2800
Liz Noone	(410) 263-6040
Sound Hound	(212) 575-8664
Voiceovers Unlimited (Dan Duckworth)	1-800-888-VEOH
VoiceWorks (Steve Garrin)	(212) 541-6592
David Zema	(212) 473-3898

San Francisco:

Voice Factory (Taylor Korobow)	(415)296-7753
VoiceTrax, San Francisco	(415) 331-8800

Virginia:

Lion & Fox Recording (Rob Burhman)	(703) 941-6100

Washington, DC/Baltimore/Philadelphia:

Liz Noone	(410) 263-6040
ROAR Media Productions, Inc. (Steven Rosch)	1-800-466-ROAR
VoiceWorks (Steve Garrin)	1-800-63-VOCAL

APPENDIX C

DEMO TAPE DUPLICATION

Chicago:

Audio One (Kirk Johnson, Sr.)	(312) 337-5111
Chicago Recording Co. (Hank Newberger)	(312) 822-9333
Streeterville (Bob Dolen)	(312) 644-1666

Los Angeles:

a t & t (Sheina Smith)	(213) 466-9000
Dynamite Dubs (Susan Palyo)	(213) 851-3850
Hollywood Recording Services	(213) 957-8400
North Hollywood Tape Duplication (Charlene Schulz)	(818) 985-9737
Norwich Studios (Ann Parr)	(818) 980-2615

Los Angeles:(continued)

Kris Stevens Enterprises (Debbie Butala)	(818) 225-7585
Rainbo Records (Jack Brown)	(310) 829-0355
Straight Copy (Tom Smart)	(818) 509-6774
Tape Specialty, Inc. (Stu Feldman)	(818) 786-6111

New York:

A & J Recording Studio (Gerald Kornbluth)	(212) 247-4860
Angel Sound (Angel Sandoval)	(212) 765-7460
Full House Productions (Jeff Bush)	(212) 645-2228
Steve Harris' The Art of Voice	(212) 517-8616
Sound Hound	(212) 575-8664
Voiceovers Unlimited (Dan Duckworth)	1-800-888-VEOH

San Francisco:

Fast Forward	(415) 989-6245
Realtime (Tony Johnson)	(415) 459-7180

Virginia:

Lion & Fox Recording (Rob Burhman)	(703) 941-6100

APPENDIX D

GRAPHICS FOR DEMO TAPE CONTAINERS

San Francisco:

Paul Costanzo & Associates	(415) 804-2569
Renolds & Renolds	(415) 252-8480

APPENDIX E

VOICE-OVER AGENCY LIST

Atlanta:

Atlanta Models & Talent, Inc. (Kathy Hardegree)	(404) 261-9627
Ted Borden & Associates	(404) 266-0664
L'Agence Models (Kitty Bundy)	(770) 396-9015
People Store (Rebecca Shrager)	(404) 874-6448

Chicago
Harrise Davidson & Associates (Jennifer McInnis)	(312) 782-4480
Shirley Hamilton (Lynne Hamilton)	(312) 787-4700
Jefferson & Associates	(312) 337-1930
Emelia Lorence, Ltd.	(312) 787-3610
Stewart Talent Management (Joan Sparks)	(312) 943-3131

Dallas/Fort Worth:
Mary Collins Agency	(214) 360-0900
Kim Dawson Talent (Silvia Gill)	(214) 630-5161

Denver:
Barbizon Agency (John Urquhart)	(303) 337-6952

Houston:
Sherry Young/ Mad Hatter, Inc. (Michael Young)	(713) 266-5800

Los Angeles:
Abrams Rubaloff & Lawrence (Lynda McCarrell)	(213) 935-1700
Bobby Ball Agency (Patty Grana Miller)	(818) 506-8188
Cassell/Levy, Inc. (Leanna Levy)	(213) 461-3971
Commercials Unlimited (Rich Reiner)	(310) 888-8788
Cunningham, Escott & Dipene	(310) 475-2111
International Creative Management (Jeff Danis)	(310) 550-4304
William Morris Agency (Nina Nisenhortz)	(310) 859-4124
Don Pitts Voices/Kazarian/Spencer & Assoc.	(818) 769-9111
Special Artists Agency (Marcia Hurwitz)	(310) 859-9688
Sutton Barth & Vennari (Rita Vennari)	(213) 938-6000
Talent Group, Inc. (West Stevens/Kama Nist/Y. Urbina)	(213) 852-9559
Herb Tannen & Associates	(213) 782-0515
Arlene Thornton & Associates	(818) 760-6688
Tisherman Agency (Steve Tisherman)	(213) 850-6767

Minneapolis:
Moore Creative Talent, Inc. (Andrea Hjelm)	(612) 375-0525
New Faces (Diane Gale)	(612) 544-8668
Susan Wehmann	(612) 333-6393

Nashville:

Chaparral Talent Agency (Kathy Carver/Theatrica v/o)	(423) 238-9790
Talent & Model Land (Betty Clark)	(615) 321-5596

New York:

Abrams Artists & Associates, Ltd. (Neal Altman)	(212) 935-8980
J. Michael Bloom (Linda Weaver)	(212) 529-6500
Don Buchwald & Associates (Scott Linder)	(212) 867-1070
Cunningham, Escott & Dipene (Billy Collura)	(212) 477-1666
International Creative Management (Celebrity)	(212) 556-5600
William Morris Agency	(212) 586-5100
Fifi Oscard Associates (Graham Murray)	(212) 764-1100
Paradigm Talent (Vickie Barroso)	(212) 246-1030

Philadelphia:

Expressions Models and Talent	(215) 923-4420

San Francisco:

Look Talent (Joan Spangler)	(415) 781-2841
Mitchell Management (Byron Peters)	(415) 395-9291
Stars, The Agency	(415) 421-6272
Voice Factory (Taylor Korobow)	(415) 296-7753

St. Louis:

The Delcia Agency (Joannie Tackette)	(314) 726-3223

Tampa/Orlando:

Berg Talent & Model (Carol Berg)	(813) 877-5533
Coconut Grove Talent	(305) 858-3002

Washington, DC/Maryland:

Central Casting (Carol Ness/Washington, DC)	(202) 547-6300
Central Casting (Baltimore)	(410) 889-3200

Glossary

"accent it" — Add stress or emphasis to your reading of a syllable, word or phrase.

active commercial — Calls for an aggressive delivery. It's also known as a "hard sell."

"add life to it" — Your reading is dead. Give it C.P.R. (Concentration, Positive energy and Revive it!)

announce booth — See "studio."

A.D.R. — Stands for "Automated Dialogue Replacement" in a film. (We've also heard it called "Automatic Dialogue Replacement.") It's a more modern technology than looping. All the sound readers and the projector are kept in absolute synch as you project forward or back up. Instead of having to do anything in one continuous take or having to cut the picture into loops, you can actually take the film as it's edited to be seen, back it up on the projector, and start replacing lines section by section. You can literally punch in any time you want to. It's a magnetic recording, and it's capable of doing a very silent job of punching in without any clicks or pops.

attitude — How your character feels about a particular product. Also, how you feel about a particular situation, be it interview, audition or job. A good attitude can get you remembered kindly all over town.

background noise — The sounds of those activities which are going on simultaneously with the spoken words of the commercial. They are either recorded live along with the copy, or are mixed in later in post.

Basic Process — Our surefire three-step method for delivering the most exciting, believable readings: Focus your energy on doing the voice-over, visualize the copy and commit to that picture of it.

"be real" — Keep your delivery as true-to-life as possible. Add a genuine or sincere quality to your character.

"billboard it" — Highlight or emphasize your reading.

break character — When you become another character or lose the one you were. Happens to the best of us when our concentration's thrown off.

"bring it up/down" — Increase/decrease the intensity of your reading. May also refer to raising or lowering your volume.

bumper — Extra recording or post time in a studio.

buy — As in "That's a buy." That take is the one they want.

buy-out — A one-time fee paid for your voice-over services. Typically seen in nonunion situations and industrials.

cadence — Having to do with how the words are strung together in phrasing; how breaks are placed in between words.

call-back — A request for you to go back for another audition. (Okay, so maybe you can't open the bottle of champagne just yet, but you can start chilling it.)

"cans" — A nickname for headphones.

character — That person you've chosen to be in a commercial. Even as an announcer, you must choose to be a Particular Announcer to do the best possible readings.

"color it" — Find the magic in the copy; give it shades of meaning.

"cones" — Another nickname for headphones.

conflict — You would be "in conflict" if you did two commercials for the same type of product. A big no-no in the industry. A conflict can also mean that you sound like someone else. Agents may turn you down because they already have a client who has your sound, and signing you would represent a conflict.

copy — The text of a commercial. Also called a "script."

control room — Where the engineer, producer, client, etc. are located during a session. Also called the "booth."

cuts through — When your voice nicely overrides the music and sound effects. It cuts through, but doesn't demolish the other effects.

dead air — What happens when a voice-over pause is too long.

demo — A demonstration tape of your talent. A sales tool, it serves as your remote audition for agents and casting people.

dialogue — The words in the ad copy.

double — A commercial calling for two characters. Also called a "two-person spot."

donut — Copy at the beginning and/or the end of a spot. It "wraps around" the body of the commercial, which changes from spot to spot while the donut is always the same. Example: "And now at Donna's Discount Delight ... (body of the commercial) ... New for you from Donna's."

drop — Lowering the volume or intensity of the reading.

dry mouth — What you get when you've been at the mike too long, or because your nerves are acting up.

dubbing — Dubbing really has nothing to do with replacing dialogue tracks. It is actually the process of mixing down the picture or the spot, and it's something the engineers do once the voice-over talent has gone home. Over the years, however, dubbing has become synonymous with looping. Some people also refer to the dialogue replacement in a foreign film as dubbing.

edge — The quality your voice takes on when you intensify your attitude.

"endow the copy" — Using our Basic Process to give the copy a special something which will make it your very own.

energy age — The age you "think" so that your character, regardless of his or her chronological age, can always give a fresh reading.

equalizer — A machine with treble and bass controls. Engineers use it to thin out or give bottom end to your voice, which can make your character seem, for example, more important or sexier.

fade-in/fade-out — What happens to the sound of your voice when you turn your head away from the mike and back again while you are speaking.

"Father Clarity" — (This is not someone who is called in to administer the last rites to dead air.) Often directors ask talent to watch their diction. Out of numerous requests to "read the copy with more clarity" has come the short-hand expression, "Father Clarity."

"fix it in the mix" — When mistakes are not handled or caught while the talent is still in the studio, the engineers must correct them in post.

fluctuation — How often your voice goes up and down. If you have no fluctuation in your voice, you are speaking in a monotone.

Folley stage — A special sound stage used for source sound effects. Boards on a Folley stage floor may be raised to provide access to areas filled with different substances, such as loose gravel, sand or pavement. Various props may also be found on a Folley stage. The process itself involves watching on-screen characters and matching appropriate noises to their actions. Footsteps, glass breaking, doors and windows opening and closing are all examples of noises that can be produced on a Folley stage. (Susan once saw someone working on a Folley stage, and as he walked across it, he had his hand cupped to his ear like Gary Owens!)

gate — Another name for dialect.

"give me a level" — Start reading your copy exactly the way you plan to read it for an actual take. This is done so the engineer can adjust the equipment to best record your voice.

go up for — To audition or be considered for a job. "I went up for a 'Curry's Department Store,'" means you auditioned for that spot. "I'm up for a 'Wagner's Dog Food,'" means you already auditioned and they are now considering you for that spot.

hard sell — See "active commercial."

"highpoint" — The last beat or resolution to the mini-play that is in a piece of copy.

hold — You are "on hold" when you are being paid not to do certain types of spots because the spot you recorded has yet to run and would be in conflict with the others.

house tape — An agency's demo. It includes condensed versions of the clients' demos, usually separated into male and female sections.

inflection — The raising or lowering of the pitch of your voice. Generally used for longer phrases, rather than a one- or two-word ad.

intensity — A focusing of your energy that is reflected in your character's attitude.

"keep it fresh" — When you're reading the copy for the twenty-fifth time, give it the energy of your very first take.

laundry list — When there are lots of adjectives in a piece of copy.

lay it down — Record a piece of copy.

"less sell" — Make it a softer spot.

live mike — The mike is on. And can pick up anything you say. And will deliver it straight to the ears of the producer, the engineer, the clients and anyone else who is crammed into the control room. (And it may come back to haunt you, as it did Susan. She used to spit out some interesting four-letter words when she flubbed a line. When she went to an important client's Christmas party, they played a tape of her "outtakes." "I almost died of embarrassment," she says. "Now I watch my mouth.")

live tag — One or two-line copy delivered live by a D.J. at the end of a pre-recorded spot.

looping — The older technology of dialogue replacement in a film. A scene is cut into pieces, each piece being the length of a particular line. The pieces are joined into loops and mounted on a projector so you, as the looping talent, can see them over and over. You look at the screen and it's black. Then a white line runs across it from screen left to screen right. When it hits the right edge of the screen, the scene will come up. You'll hear and see how the original line was spoken. At the end of that line, you'll go back to black and the white line will again make its way across the screen. This enables you to establish a matching rhythm to what you are looping.

major markets — Cities such as Los Angeles, Chicago and New York, where the majority of voice-over work takes place.

"make it flow" — Make your delivery smooth. Avoid choppy, staccato readings.

"make it intimate" — Do you really need us to tell you what this means?

"make it yours" — Personalize the copy. Endow it.

mix — The result of a mix-down.

mix-down — Combining the various voice, sound effects and music tracks into one.

"more energy" — Punch it up — you're dragging your vocal tush.

"more sell" — Billboard the copy.

multiple — A commercial calling for more than two characters.

nerves — As in "I've got a bad case of ...." They usually start doing their thing before an interview, an audition or a job. They are something to leave outside the door when you go in for the interview, audition or job. Your best bet is to turn them into positive energy and let them work for you.

one-on-one — See "intimate."

overlapping — In a double (or multiple), starting your line a fraction of a second before your partner finishes his or hers.

pace — The speed with which you read the copy.

paper noise — The mike can pick up the sound if you move your copy — put it on a script stand!

passive commercial — A soft sell. It calls for a more laid-back approach.

pause — A break in-between syllables, words or phrases. Remember to make it a short break or you'll have dead air.

phase interference — What happens when sound reflects off your script and into the mike.

phonemes — Very small units of the sounds we use to make up words. Example: the "r" of the word "rat."

"pick up your cue" — Come in faster on a particular line.

pick-up session — An additional taping to record individual lines out of context either for backup protection or because they weren't right the first time — for whatever reason. Sometimes an entire script may have to be redone.

pitch — The up's and down's we hear in normal conversation. The musical level at which you speak.

placement — Where the voice is coming from, i.e. the nose, the chest, the stomach, etc.

pop filter — Styrofoam balls that fit over the mike to eliminate pops.

pops — Noises resulting from hard consonants spoken directly into the mike. They sound like short, sharp bursts from an air gun.

post — The post-production session that starts once the voice-over talent has completed the recording session.

pre-life — What was going on with your character just before the actual copy starts.

promo — A promotional spot. It promotes a product or, more often, a service.

"punch it" — Give the copy more energy.

"push/don't push" — Give the copy more/less energy.

read against the text — Reading a line with an emotion other than the one it would ordinarily call for.

residuals — Continuing payments you receive each time your spot is run. Usually divided into thirteen-week cycles.

rhythm — The cadence of the speaking voice.

"romance the 'phone" — Make friends with that mike. It is your only link to that particular person you're speaking to.

run-through — Rehearsal of the copy before an actual take is done.

scale — The established union wage rate for a recording session.

S.A.S.E. — Self-addressed, stamped envelope.

"sell it" — Billboard or punch it.

session — A recording session. The period of time in a studio during which the voice-over talent lays down the copy.

SFX — Stands for "sound effects."

"shave it by ..." — Cut a certain amount of time off your delivery.

signature — Your vocal signature are those qualities which make your voice unmistakably yours.

single — Copy calling for just one character. Also called "one-person copy."

"slate your name" — Before doing the take, record your name.

smile — As in "Remember to ...." And you'll warm up the copy, the casting director, the agent, the producer, the client, the engineer, yourself, and maybe a few others who have the good fortune to catch your smile.

soft sell — See "passive commercial."

"spokes" — Short for spokesperson.

station I.D. — Very short spot in which the call letters of a particular radio or TV station are announced.

steps — Increasing the punch (energy) on each adjective when copy includes a long list of them.

step on lines — What happens when you overlap your partner's line by starting your own reading too soon.

storyboard — An artist's rendering of each camera set-up. A storyboard often accompanies the advertising copy so that talent can see what the on-camera actors will be doing in the spot.

studio — Room in which the talent actually records the copy. It's sometimes called the "announce booth."

tags — Short one- or two-line pieces of copy that either end a spot or stand alone to identify and describe the product.

take — The recording of a piece of copy. The original recording is Take 1; others follow in numerical sequence.

talk-back — The mike(s) over which the producer speaks to the talent in the studio. It's also used when the producer or engineer in the control room slates your name for you.

"talk to me" — Make your delivery more conversational.

tempo — How slowly or quickly you speak.

"throw it away" — Don't put any stress or emphasis on the reading. Make it light.

tone — Sound quality of the voice. Harsh, sexy, nasal, etc.

under/over — As in "You were ...." Your delivery was either too short or too long, and didn't come in exactly on time.

"underscore it" — Highlight it.

units — Small voice-over market areas

vocal characterization sheet — Developed by Pat Fraley. A form on which you can record your individual characters.

voice-over hangover — The escalating doubts and fears which hit just after an audition. Take two positives and call your Mom in the morning.

voice prints — The vocal equivalent of fingerprints. Using samples of phonemes, experts can make positive identifications of speakers.

volume — How loudly something is said.

"warm up the copy" — Make your delivery friendlier or more intimate.

wild line — A line recorded during a pick-up session.

windscreen — A pop filter.

PLEASE SEND ME THE FOLLOWING

Copies of **WORD OF MOUTH**-The Guide To
Commercial Voice-over Excellence-(This Book)
ISBN 0938817-32-9   **$11.95** each copy

Copies of **WORD OF MOUTH** Audio Cassette
ISBN 0938817-09-4   **$11.95** each cassette

Fifty-minute audio cassette with exercises, sample
advertising copy, professional demos and audition
material featuring top voice-over artists.

NAME:_____

ADDRESS:_____

CITY:_____STATE:_____ZIP:_____

TELEPHONE:(_____)_____

California residents please add 8.25% ($ .99) sales tax for each item.

Shipping and handling $3.50 for 1 or 2 items, 3-day priority mail service.

TOTAL AMOUNT ENCLOSED: $_____._____

Make check or money order payable to: Pomegranate Press, Ltd.
and mail with this order form or a photocopy to:

Pomegranate Press, Ltd.

Post Office Box 17217

Beverly Hills, California 90209-3217